# Affiliate Marketing

## The Ultimate Guide to a Profitable Online Business

By

Nik Neutron

*Nik Neutron*

# Table of Contents

*Nik Neutron*

*Nik Neutron*

Respective authors own all copyrights not held by the publisher.

The information herein is offered for informational purposes solely and is universal as so. The presentation of the information is without a contract or any type of guarantee assurance.

# Introduction

I want to thank you for choosing this book, *"Affiliate Marketing - The Ultimate Guide to a Profitable Online Business"* and hope you find the book informative and interesting. After the tremendous success of the first edition of this book, I have compiled more information, together with examples, to give you an even more in-depth understanding of the topic.

Whether people are looking to just diversify their income or pursue a whole new career, the idea of pulling in money online has been gaining more and more traction with many folks all over the world. The prospect of passive income has also become more appealing than ever, thanks to the wonders of the Internet and many other new technologies. This is because the Internet's growth throughout the globe has not only brought about the emergence of many new businesses but has also bolstered existing ones. Quite a few sectors have changed in recent times and will never be the same again.

Once upon a time, one had to own real estate or a well-established company with employees in order to enjoy some sort of passive income, but this is no longer the case. Nowadays, online content creators and many other folks are raking in considerable bucks from many sides, both actively and passively, through all sorts of ventures, one of which is the growing affiliate marketing sector. While affiliate marketing can be a good way for publishers, artists, and various content creators to passively acquire some additional income, one can also make this a full-time business and grow it significantly.

Of course, marketing has been an integral part of many business ventures ever since folks first decided to sell their articles publicly. However, marketing is a very broad term that encompasses quite a few different methods and even entire industries, one of which is affiliate marketing. You may have heard about it just in passing, talked to someone who made his or her riches through it, or read a blog post about it, but this book will help you broaden your horizons, get a better idea of what affiliate marketing is, and, of course, explain how you can get in on this potentially lucrative business endeavor.

Depending on what you do for a living right now and whether you have experience in some form of online business, success in affiliate marketing might require you to put in a lot of effort at first, but it might also be just a decision away. We will explore the essence of what affiliate marketing is, what its benefits are, and the many ways of going about it, so even if you are completely clueless on the matter, you will be able to see whether this business is right for you and what the best approach for you would be.

What's certain is that affiliate marketing is no empty promise and no scheme that proposes to make you a millionaire overnight. It is a very real and serious prospect of earning money and, as such, requires a very serious and decisive approach if you are to see concrete results. This doesn't mean that it's particularly difficult, but it does mean that you shouldn't expect to get rich immediately without lifting a finger. Besides, schemes that do promise you these overnight riches are virtually always scams, and affiliate marketing is everything but.

Affiliate marketing is a talent-based marketing program where one is compensated for every buyer brought in by the affiliate's own effort. It usually includes four major factors: the merchant, the network, the publisher, and the buyer. The merchant is also known as the brand or the retailer, and the network is from where the affiliate chooses an offer from and deals with revenue.

The publisher is known as the affiliate and the buyer is referred to as the customer who purchases the product. This style of marketing has become more complex over the years and has resulted in a secondary level of affiliates known as super affiliates, third-party vendors, and affiliate management firms. Internet business methods get overlapped by affiliate marketing to a certain degree because regular advertising methods such as email marketing, content marketing, advertisements, SEO, and paid search engine marketing, are used by affiliates. Other methods, such as review publication of a product or service, are also used.

Most advertising companies will hire an affiliate network to track their affiliate campaigns. The network will give them a set of links that are trackable to the affiliates; these links are embedded to their banners and tests on the affiliate's website. When a customer clicks on the link, it is registered by the affiliate network. When the customer makes a purchase, it reaches the advertiser's confirmation page. The customer is then put under the scanner to see if he or she came from a specific affiliate networks publisher. Both the advertiser and affiliate will be able to see that the sale has been made, and a commission will be given. This book will help you understand the different strategies that can be used to make your online business a success. Enjoy reading!

# FREE AFFILIATE MARKETING TRAINING REVEALS...

## Secrets From 15 Bona Fide Super Affiliates

### LET ME INTRODUCE YOU TO YOUR

# DREAM TEAM

**Meet The Team & Get Their Proven Step-By-Step Methods ...FREE**

www.freedomfightersacademy.com
/affiliate-marketing-training/

# Chapter One: What is Affiliate Marketing?

If you're completely new to this concept, the idea might take some getting used to, but, in due time, you will find that the underlying principles of affiliate marketing are not that hard to grasp. In essence, affiliate marketing is a two-sided marketing effort that includes three to four layers or parties, depending on the definition. It is generally defined as a process where you, as the affiliate, earn commissions from each sale you facilitate by promoting a product line or service that someone else provides to a select market. In order to truly understand what affiliate marketing is, though, you need to become acquainted with all the parties and components involved in the process and learn what each of them has to invest and stands to gain in the end.

We will explore the benefits of affiliate marketing in more detail in our next chapter, but one of the defining characteristics of this business is its accessibility to a layperson. That is, you don't need to be a marketing expert or a multi-billion-dollar marketing company to do it. Before affiliate marketing exploded on the Internet, marketing as a whole was an industry reserved for major companies that specialized in creating and spreading advertisements for their clients, often through multi-million-dollar contracts.

While the traditional aspects of this industry are still very much in place, such methods as affiliate marketing have diverged from the mainstream and opened up opportunities for virtually anyone with Internet access. Not only that, but the manufacturers, service providers, and other sellers will often prefer to use affiliates to market their products as opposed to spending a lot of money on ads that may or may not work or even reach their potential customers. Major businesses that do spend millions on marketing will also use affiliates to boost their sales even further. As such, affiliate marketing has essentially become universally utilized, with some of the biggest companies on the planet using it extensively.

An affiliate marketing venture is a relationship between two sides, namely, you, as the publisher or owner of an online platform (in the broadest sense), and a company, brand, or individual that has something to sell. In the interest of simplicity, let us consider an example. Imagine a successful YouTube channel that revolves around reviewing power tools, video games, or PC hardware and has a considerable audience that tunes in regularly and relies on this channel's reviews to help make the right purchases.

Such YouTube channels have multiple ways through which they can monetize their success, and most of these methods revolve around advertising, but not all of them are affiliate marketing. Most YouTube channels, including smaller ones, will enroll in a partnership program with a website and display various ads on their content, drawing income through Google AdSense. This income is based on such factors as clicks and other interactions between the advertised product and the channel's audience. The amount of money that you can earn in this manner can greatly vary and depends on the amount of traffic your channel receives and generates for the advertiser; thus, the arrangement works out best for major channels. This is a decent way to simply allow YouTube to use your videos for advertising and handle the whole deal while you, as the channel's owner, don't have to do much of anything.

However, with just a bit more effort, by engaging in affiliate marketing, these channels can make much more money. The aforementioned review channels can thus choose to present a certain product, brand, website, and much else to their viewers. As such, these channels will essentially refer their audience to a brand of their choosing, and every sale that results from these referrals will yield a commission for the channel, which can be as high as 15% to 20%, and sometimes even higher. This is the very core of affiliate marketing.

The way this is usually done is through a unique link or referral code that, when used, will leave a cookie on a customer's browser and allow the vendor to track the source of the traffic, knowing that a particular affiliate is the one to thank and pay for the sale. Usually, sales made through your link will yield a commission, even if the customer made the purchase a while after visiting the article for the first time. This window can vary depending on the different arrangements and parties in the equation.

Referral codes are usually given to affiliates who, in turn, provide these codes to their audience to use for discounts, cheaper subscriptions, and the like. As you can probably imagine, of course, a tool or computer hardware review channel will almost always strike a deal with a vendor or manufacturer that sells products that are relevant to these respective niches. If a channel reviews video games, the owner will naturally market video games or game-selling platforms to his or her audience, who will show interest in the product. That means accuracy and effectiveness in advertising, which is why affiliate marketing is so popular.

This also brings us to one important fact, which is that an affiliate doesn't necessarily have to sell or market a product per se. Sometimes, websites of all kinds will just want to generate more traffic to help them grow, and they will do this by acquiring affiliates that will promote their website to their online followers and other contacts. In this type of arrangement, the system usually revolves around small payments per action, which can be whenever a new user, as referred to the website by you, signs up for an account, subscribes to the site's email newsletter, and so on. While it may not be as lucrative or commonplace in the world of affiliate marketing as shared revenue through sales, this is certainly an approach worth considering.

As you begin forming a better idea of what affiliate marketing is, one burning question usually arises: How exactly does one go about forming this relationship with a brand and becoming an affiliate? We will explore many different ways and the details thereof later in this book, but for now, it's important to distinguish between two main ways of establishing your affiliate relationship. The first way is to either wait for a brand or store to approach you, which happens very often for growing online publishers and content creators, or to approach someone yourself. Another method is through the many affiliate marketing networks or platforms that exist online, some of which have become enormous and incredibly profitable. All of these and much more will become clearer as we move along.

All this is to say that affiliate marketing is a way for you to share in the revenue of sales without contributing to the production, design, or anything of that nature. Even the marketing you will be doing is not particularly active and demanding, as it leans more toward the realm of passive. As you have probably begun to understand by now, however, affiliate marketing is also intertwined with an online presence. Keep in mind that we used YouTube only as an example, but it's only one of the many platforms where affiliate marketing is booming.

We'll look into all of the major platforms and fields in more detail later on, but suffice it to say that affiliate marketing is an option for website owners, bloggers, social media personalities and pages, various artists and other content creators, and many others. It's all about developing and growing an online presence or platform and then monetizing it through the clever advertising of the products and services that you choose.

We also mentioned that affiliate marketing is a three- or four-party arrangement. As you probably gathered by now, these are the vendor or manufacturer, the affiliate or publisher, and the potential customer or consumer. The fourth party is an affiliate network or platform that deals in connecting vendors and affiliates with mutual interests and helps facilitate their business. The reason that this fourth piece of the puzzle is only sometimes used in the definition is that it's up to the affiliates and brands to decide whether they want to use such platforms at all.

*Nik Neutron*

# Chapter Two: Benefits of Affiliate Marketing

We briefly mentioned in the previous chapter that affiliate marketing is not particularly demanding, and this is definitely the first benefit to consider as a potential affiliate marketer, especially if you are still on the fence. As the affiliate, your responsibility essentially boils down to producing traffic and attracting interest, but the thing about affiliate marketing is that it usually goes hand in hand with online content creation. What this means for you is that, if you are a content creator, running a website, or have any other form of online following, the interest is already there. Beyond that, it's only a matter of introducing your audience to the right product using the right approach.

As an affiliate marketer, you don't really manufacture anything, come up with fancy marketing ideas, design products, or do any legwork. All you have to do is give people a nudge and push them in the right direction, and if you are an established online figure, page, or channel, that should be a piece of cake. If that online presence is already established, getting started in affiliate marketing will take no time at all. This is because, beyond building your base and amassing an audience, setting up an affiliate program for yourself requires almost no investment when it comes to your time.

In affiliate marketing, your number one capital is your audience. Think of it like a check waiting to be cashed in, with cashing in being the work you have to do. The work, however, does not revolve just around building up a following and striking any affiliate deal you can get your hands on. The second major ingredient in successful affiliate marketing is integrity. This means that you need to be careful which products you will promote, how often, and in what way. Some affiliate marketers choose to be very transparent with their audiences, always letting them know when a particular product or service is being promoted for a commission. This is especially important for blogs, channels, and websites that deal in reviews, where the publisher would be well-advised to make it clear whether a post is a promotion or an impartial review.

While there's nothing inherently wrong with keeping this on the down low, viewers and readers will appreciate your openness if you do choose to be transparent. The potential to foster this trusting relationship and make it work for you is another major benefit of affiliate marketing. Most people don't really care for ads on the Internet or anywhere else, which is why traditional advertising so frequently relies on saturation. It's often based on a "spray and pray" principle of producing as many ads as possible and inflating their presence so as to reach as many folks as possible, with only a hope that some of them will listen. Affiliate marketing is quite the opposite.

That is, affiliate marketing is all about niches and quality, well-orientated marketing. This is why such marketing is also incredibly beneficial for the sellers themselves. Advertising will have a much higher rate of success if a product is being marketed to a select group or demographic directly and through a source they already know and trust.

The third party, made up of the customers or your audience, will also benefit from affiliate marketing. For one, they will be getting product recommendations from a trusted source, as opposed to seeing them on a billboard. If you, as an online tech reviewer, for example, recommend or positively review a certain piece of hardware, a loyal reader or viewer will be much more inclined to buy it. Furthermore, as we briefly mentioned, vendors will often give their affiliates various special links or referral codes to forward to their followers, which can grant them many great perks, such as free trials, discounts, and many other privileges. Therefore, affiliate marketing is often a true win-win situation for all the parties involved.

Something else to keep in mind is that you don't really have to be an expert on the product or service that you are promoting. We talked about being a publisher in a specific niche and promoting fully relevant products, but that's not necessarily how you must do it. There are many products and services that are marketable on various platforms that may not have anything to do with the niche at first glance. To that end, a tech reviewer could also become an affiliate of a website that offers web courses in languages, IT, and so on. There is no written rule that says that you have to adhere to your niche a hundred percent — some things are just universally interesting and useful to potential customers.

Furthermore, some companies or websites aren't necessarily selling anything to begin with. As the affiliate, you could be asked to incentivize your audience to visit a certain site and boost their traffic. We mentioned earlier that this is usually done through a unique link, with earnings paid via a cost per action system, but you can also do it for a fee or an agreed upon rate. That would still be affiliate marketing. Furthermore, even free services could be promoted for money by affiliates, but it all depends on what the other side wants.

What's also great about being an affiliate marketer is that you are, in a way, selling things, but you don't have to worry about a single aspect of logistics the way that you would have to when you are involved in actual sales. Shipping will have absolutely nothing to do with you, and neither will customer support. If a customer ends up unsatisfied with a product or service, your reputation with that person could be damaged, but solving such problems will fall on the vendor. Moreover, after a purchase has turned sour, many customers will rightfully blame the vendor or manufacturer, not you. Your involvement in the financial side of things will also be minimal, as the vendor will usually take care of everything, including getting the money to you directly or through your affiliate network. All that's left for you to do is cash in and look through your financial reports to track your progress.

Of course, another crucial benefit of affiliate marketing is its incredibly high income ceiling. This is one of those businesses where you can rake in anywhere between ten bucks per month to millions of dollars every year, and with the low risks and investments required, affiliate marketing is quite an opportune field as long as you make the right choices.

Last but definitely not the least, an affiliate marketer is his or her own boss. Many of the people who turn to this revenue stream are individuals who have become fed up with the nine-to-five office job routine, and chances are good that you are one of them. In fact, successful affiliate marketers usually manage their own time in a way that suits them best, and, if they make the right choices, they often end up doing something they truly love while acquiring more than enough passive income to live comfortably. This is, perhaps, the greatest benefit of affiliate marketing, as it can mean freedom, great independence, and a lot of fulfillment that many traditionally employed folks yearn for.

# Chapter Three: Low Ticket, High Ticket, and Recurring Affiliate Marketing

Before we proceed with the actual steps that you must take to get started in affiliate marketing, we have one last essential topic to cover, and it concerns the cornerstone of the business — commissions. Commissions are the alpha and omega, the bread and butter for every affiliate marketer, and they can work in a couple of different ways. Some of these ways of making a commission will work better in one niche than another.

**Low-ticket affiliate marketing** usually refers to the promotion of cheaper products that are expected to sell en masse. These can be things like books and courses, or even cheaper articles like t-shirts, small household items, and the like. As these products are cheap, the companies that produce them can be very conservative with the commissions that they will grant their affiliates. As such, low-ticket affiliate marketing is sometimes seen as being quite a grind. If you, as an affiliate, want to rake in thousands of dollars every month via small commissions on cheap products, you will have to refer a lot of sales to your partner.

While such deals may be easy to find, they can be a difficult way of making money for a fresh affiliate, such as you. This is especially the case if your online platform is still growing and doesn't pull in thousands upon thousands of viewers and visitors every day. If a YouTube channel, for example, has hundreds of thousands or even millions of subscribers, low-ticket deals can indeed be quite lucrative and come easy, but as a rookie, you want higher commissions on hefty individual sales. Simply put, why facilitate two-hundred sales in a month if you can make the same amount of money or more via twenty or less? Even better, as a large platform, why make $20,000 through your 200,000 subscribers if you can make $70,000 with fewer sales?

One of the few advantages of low-ticket affiliate products is that, due to their cheapness, it will be easier for you to sell them. It doesn't take much convincing to get someone with a credit card to buy a 6-dollar mug with a funny catchphrase written on it. This is why many new affiliate marketers choose this route when they are just starting out, but some of them end up underestimating the difficulty of selling hundreds of products every month and overestimating their audience's interest. All of this can lead to a lot of work for less than ideal pay, and it can even discourage beginners from pursuing this whole venture any further.

The aforementioned lucrative alternative is known as **high-ticket sales or affiliate marketing**. This is simply the opposite of low ticket, as explained above, and essentially, all affiliates would be well-advised to pursue these types of deals, if possible, regardless of experience. What's great about high-ticket affiliate products is that if you establish yourself as their marketer right from the start, and your income will grow exponentially as your platform begins drawing in more visitors. Some high-ticket products will be so expensive, and their sellers could give you such good commissions, that just one or two sales could be all you need to make thousands of dollars more each month.

One thing that you should understand, however, is that if you are only about to begin building your online platform to use for affiliate marketing, the decision between high- and low-ticket sales can wait. This will be much clearer over the next two chapters, but for now, let's just say that there are much more important things to focus on while you're still amassing an audience. The right approach for you, as well as its feasibility, will depend on many different factors, such as your niche and the type of content you will produce.

If you decide to review books on your blog or page because you love to read, chances are good that you will end up relying largely on low-ticket marketing. Of course, bookworms can promote much more than just the books themselves, such as various subscriptions, library memberships, writing courses, collector's items, and so on. Some of these things might indeed provide high-ticket opportunities.

Things like subscriptions and memberships bring us to the concept of **recurring affiliate marketing.** This term stems from something called a recurring commission, which, in the simplest terms, is a type of commission that's paid to you multiple times on a single sale or, more precisely, a single referral. Products and services that can yield a recurring commission for you can range widely, but what they have in common would be paid subscriptions of different kinds.

For instance, say you are running a blog about guns, frequented by many enthusiasts who care about the niche, and you stumble upon a monthly gun magazine that's looking for affiliates to promote them. By referring a reader of yours to the magazine's site and having them subscribe there once, you unlock the potential for monthly commissions from that single referral, as long as the customer keeps subscribing.

There is also software that requires regular subscriptions, various websites that provide tutorials and online classes, companies that ship prebuilt packages to subscribed customers, and many more. Subscriptions can sometimes be weekly instead of monthly, but they can also be annual. Seeing as annual subscriptions usually cost more, these types of partnerships can be seen as high-ticket recurring affiliate marketing gigs, and they can be a really good way of making money.

With all that being said, diversity is the mother of lucrative and stable income. As you can imagine, the most successful affiliate marketers will make full use of all of these types of commissions and sales. If their low-ticket ventures experience a fall during a particular month, their promotions that fall under the other two categories might increase. Obviously, there doesn't have to be a correlation there, but the point is that the risk is minimized by putting your eggs into three baskets.

# Chapter Four: How to Become an Affiliate Marketer

By now, you should have a very clear idea of what affiliate marketing is and who it is best suited for. As you may have noticed, this gig works best for those who have an online presence, which refers to that "audience capital" that we mentioned. If you are one of these folks and are ready to give affiliate marketing a go, it's just a matter of taking that step and starting to make your online platform truly work for you.

This is why affiliate marketing, in and of itself, is fairly straightforward and easy, but getting started with it might take quite a bit of effort for some, and if you don't run a blog, a YouTube channel, a website, or have a considerable social media following, you will be among those who'll have to put in the work and start from scratch. Simply put, you need a place of your own where you can engage in affiliate marketing.

Do not be alarmed, though, as just because you're a regular anonymous on the Internet doesn't mean that affiliate marketing is not for you. After all, everyone had to start from scratch at some point. In this chapter, we will look at some of the most famous platforms on the Internet where those with an audience can monetize that human capital and how exactly they could go about it.

## Blogs

As a blogger hoping to make money through affiliate marketing, your first and immediate concern is drawing traffic to your blog. Building an audience is an absolute priority, and everything else will come later. We will go into more detail on how to produce quality content later, but, with blogs specifically, you will want to use a combination of strategies.

Some bloggers simply start out by writing about things they care about without even thinking about revenue, as sometimes, it just starts as a hobby. On the other hand, some folks go into blogging with the sole intention of engaging in affiliate marketing later. Either way, if you are to monetize your platform, you have to pick the right niche and offer something valuable. Sometimes, the value is in the information provided, but some bloggers can also gain a following because of their wit, humor, or some other quality that readers appreciate.

Either way, you just need to decide on what you want to write about, pick a blogging platform, find a host, and choose a domain name, ideally something catchy. Tools like WordPress will be your greatest asset in establishing a quality blog. As for gathering a following, you can also use advertising to promote your blog if you have a bit of money to invest. After that, it's only a matter of choosing the product or service you want to promote, which can be done through your own research or by joining an affiliate network, which we'll cover later.

# YouTube

We have mentioned YouTube quite a few times up to this point, and that was for a good reason. This platform is one of the most popular ways of acquiring affiliate marketing income in the world today.

Similar to blogs, you need to come up with an idea for what kind of content you can produce based on your skills and interests that is also in demand in the community. Tutorials and reviews are always in high demand, but so are comedy, gaming, politics, and much more.

Acquainting yourself with YouTube's algorithms and community will help you determine the best way to produce popular content in your specific niche. The thing about YouTube, though, is that consistency and frequent uploads are favored. You shouldn't underestimate the amount of work that can go into building up and running a successful YouTube channel. However, if you review things like mobile phones and include affiliate links for purchasing these phones in the descriptions of your videos, you can make a whole lot of money via commissions, depending on the size of your audience, of course, so the potential is incredible.

# Social Media

Social media websites and social networks like Facebook, Instagram, and Pinterest are also major platforms for affiliate marketing. Facebook, for example, is home to many enormous pages that can pull in a lot of money by promoting affiliate products. Facebook is also useful as a means of promoting your own blog or website by having a community page that represents it. This will also make it easier for your readers to follow you, as they will see every new post of yours on their feed.

There are also brands, content creators, and mere individuals who have millions of followers on Instagram, which is something that they monetize to great avail. Many Instagram stars enjoy lucrative sponsorship deals, but affiliate marketing is also common. A nice thing about places like Instagram and Pinterest is that you can easily create simple, individual posts to promote particular products. Instead of writing a whole blog, you can simply post a picture and a bit of text to explain what you are presenting. With a big enough audience, affiliate marketing can be a breeze on these platforms.

## Email Marketing

Whether you find yourself running a website or writing a blog, acquiring a large email list of your followers is always a welcome prospect and can be quite a useful tool. Publishers will usually do this by simply asking their visitors to provide their email addresses. This can be done on your website or blog through subscribing to your email newsletter, signing up for free accounts, participating in free surveys, and so on. Email lists are useful because they allow you to get in touch with your most loyal followers directly and, of course, use that to introduce them to products and services they may find useful.

Email lists can also be bought, although the return on that investment may be less than satisfactory. When you establish yourself in a specific niche and acquire a following, the email addresses provided to you by your visitors will be much, much more useful and valuable. Many people who start receiving emails, newsletters, and promotions from someone they never subscribed to will just unsubscribe and go about their business.

Keep in mind that, once again, diversification is the key to growth. Successful affiliate marketers with a large online presence will virtually always run at least two or three different social media pages, channels, blogs, and the like. You are sure to have noticed this if you are even remotely interested in YouTube content. Successful channels will make it possible and ask their subscribers to follow them on Twitter or Instagram, just like their Facebook page. All of these help them grow their network, gain more contacts, and expand their audience. Most importantly, it allows them to strike numerous affiliate deals with many brands across multiple platforms. For many publishers, this is the real goal of managing all these pages. An Instagram account is hardly necessary for a YouTuber to keep fans updated, but they choose to do it both to increase interaction and grow their affiliate marketing income.

Of course, it's fair to ask if it's even possible to produce so much content and manage such an expansive business successfully, and the truth is that it may require a lot of time and commitment. Clearly, the more you have to work, the less of a passive income your venture becomes. Affiliate marketing isn't a completely passive source of income to begin with, but once you grow past a certain point, new opportunities will open up for you. When your financial situation becomes more stable, and you start looking for ways to invest some of your income, you can consider hiring help not only to manage your pages but also to contribute to them, if you trust the person you hire. As time goes by, you will find yourself more and more in the position of being your own boss and eventually running an entire brand, and that's something to be proud of.

*Nik Neutron*

# Chapter Five: Useful Skills for Success in Affiliate Marketing

As we already mentioned, affiliate marketing is a highly accessible business that doesn't require much skill to get started. The industry is filled with incredibly successful individuals who started slow and small and who had a very limited skillset when they started.

Over time, these folks have consistently honed their skills and improved in many areas, and it is this willingness to learn and grow that is responsible for their success in this field of work. As with any other business, however, there are quite a few skills that will be incredibly useful even before you begin, and they might just give you the edge that you need. In this chapter, we will explore a few of these skills, and you might find that you already possess some of them.

Of course, if your business grows to a certain point, it will also be possible to hire a few people for some of the tasks. Experienced affiliate marketers do this all the time, as some prefer to get others on board to compensate for their lack of particular skills. This allows these affiliates to focus their energy on improving other skills while not missing out on opportunities to grow the business. Eventually, many affiliates will work with a whole team of people.

## Creativity

Of course, no matter what type of content they produce and publish, content creators are all about creativity, so it follows that creativity plays a major role in successful affiliate marketing. Still, the utility of creative thinking goes far beyond just the process of content creation. Success in affiliate marketing greatly depends on your ability to strategize, visualize, and come up with original ideas on how to tap into certain niches or convince your audience to check out your offers and promotions.

Affiliate marketers can get started on this venture by taking notes from others and following existing paths, but that will only get them so far. Once you start innovating, improvising, and coming up with original, creative ideas, then you will truly start to grow. Creativity is something we all possess deep down, and it's a trait that can be exercised and improved over time.

## Problem-Solving

Creativity involves problem-solving as well, which you will have to do plenty of throughout your affiliate marketing career. There will be so many instances in which problem-solving will prove crucial that it's impossible to list them all. This is especially the case because of the many different ways that individual affiliates can approach their work and construct their business model. Whatever happens within your career, you should strive to perfect your problem-solving skills as soon as possible if you feel they are lacking.

If you aren't confident in your problem-solving abilities, you can certainly help yourself by reading a plethora of books on this subject, as well as taking classes and courses that can help young entrepreneurs immensely.

## Data Analysis

As an affiliate marketer, you will be facing a whole lot of data all the time, pertaining to many different aspects of your performance. This data itself will be a crucial tool to help you adjust your approach, optimize your promotional strategy, and ultimately improve your performance.

In general, content creators have a wide range of valuable data at their disposal concerning the traffic they are receiving: how much of it, when, in what pattern, and much more. Similarly, affiliates can use various useful tools to keep track of their statistics when it comes to the sales they generate. This valuable data will teach you what group is the most responsive to your marketing, when is the best time to promote a certain product, how to go about it, and so much more. After a while, you can hire someone else to do this crucial task, but reading the data is something that you'll certainly get better at over time.

## Marketing

Marketing skills are very useful for affiliates, which is certainly a no-brainer. If you have no education or professional experience in marketing, then there's a lot that you can learn about this craft to help you become more convincing and generate more sales.

Apart from courses and classes, there are also countless books that deal with the psychological and other aspects of people's purchasing decisions. In combination with knowing the products you promote and the habits of your audience, this knowledge will help you create more effective ads and promotion pieces as well. Copywriting is another skill that's especially useful for successful marketing in today's digital environment. Keep in mind that although you won't be working as a salesperson per se, sales skills can only improve your affiliate career.

## Financial Management

First of all, knowing how to manage your money properly is the cornerstone of success in any business venture, and affiliate marketing is no different. You must be diligent in keeping track of every bit of your revenue and all of your business expenses at all times. Don't leave anything to chance or rough estimation.

Secondly, things can be tough when you're just starting out. It's important that you prepare yourself for certain sacrifices and remain wise in your spending. In fact, you will be best off viewing the money you earn as little more than a means to make more. Your income will not be just a reward – it will be a tool.

## People Skills

Given that most affiliate marketers work from home, you might be inclined to assume that people skills don't really play a part, but they certainly can. Going at it alone is certainly one way of doing things that many affiliate marketers adopt. Like any other business, however, affiliate marketing does give you room to form professional relationships, and these can provide you with a whole lot of useful perks, such as collaborations, joint strategies, and information sharing, among others.

Of course, your people skills will also come in handy if you eventually decide to start building a team. People skills don't just revolve around your ability to get along with others, but they also entail insight into human interactions in general. You'll be better able to predict who will get along well with whom and how to solve issues among employees.

## Diligence

To succeed, you should always strive to exercise your utmost diligence in all aspects of your business. If you have a problem with getting organized and being productive, you should try to make your days as structured as possible by creating intricate schedules. There should be a clear distinction between work hours and leisure time, and while you are working, distractions should be kept at a minimum.

This kind of regimen can be rather difficult to adhere to for some folks, but discipline is a skill that can be exercised and improved by everyone. Diligent folks who meticulously plan out their days will thrive in this business. Otherwise, working from home can become a problem.

## Overall Management

In general, affiliate marketing is yet another business where managerial skills can be incredibly useful. You mustn't underestimate the number of things you will have to juggle and manage to run a successful affiliate business. You'll have to keep track of your bank account, your valuable data, trends, offers, competition, the market, and so much more.

If you come to that point where you start hiring people, human resources management comes into play as well. As such, leadership is also important, and it is a skill that can be honed through time and experience. Leadership entails far more than just giving out assignments, though. Sometimes, conflict resolution, motivation, guidance, teaching, and many other things may come into play.

## Research

Anybody with an Internet connection can do some form of research, but this can definitely be considered a skill that should be practiced. As a prospective affiliate, you should know how to conduct quick and useful, as well as thorough, research. The Internet is crawling not just with clutter but also false information that can set you off course. You should know how to quickly sift through all of this information and always find what you need.

The more experience you have, the better you will be at navigating the web, but it's useful to learn how different search engines work, get acquainted with their algorithms, and make good use of keywords. Remember, the better you are at Internet research, the more you will understand how to get your pages and content into search results and reach new audiences.

## Internet Knowledge

This is one of the few skills that are actually necessary for affiliate marketers right from the start. If you are to embark on a successful affiliate endeavor, you must be at least somewhat Internet-savvy. This can mean a lot of things, but Internet knowledge could perhaps be divided into technical and cultural.

On the technical side of things, you should learn how to navigate the web quickly and efficiently, use the many tools that are available, create your platform, and understand how certain underlying mechanisms work. For instance, search engine optimization is a very important tool for many affiliates. If you decide to manage a blog or write other articles, learning SEO should be one of your top priorities if you are to push your content up to the top of search results on Google and elsewhere.

Many successful affiliate marketers also possess at least basic programming skills, which can be very helpful in many aspects of this business. Creating landing pages, registering domain names, as well as managing websites and blogs, among other things, are all important pieces of the affiliate marketing puzzle.

Being in touch with Internet culture and online human behavior is also much more useful than it might seem. Successful affiliates are attuned to the heartbeat of the Internet, so to speak. They understand what people like to see online, how they behave, what grabs their interest, and, most importantly, how to take advantage of these things.

## Web Design

The process of building and managing websites is not that complicated on a fundamental level, but improving those websites, getting them up to a certain standard, and making them more appealing to visitors are certainly trades to be practiced. Affiliates who run websites are well-advised to acquire at least a basic understanding of HTML to tap into the inner workings of Internet websites.

On the other hand, the visual aspect is almost as important as functionality. Various tools, such as Photoshop and Illustrator, can be mastered through countless online tutorials, which will help you a lot in the way of improving your skills. You can design your own, unique look, and people will appreciate that.

## Writing

For affiliate marketers, writing is an incredibly useful, versatile skill. Even a little bit of skill in this department can really go a long way toward improving your content and your marketing efforts. Of course, bloggers, article writers, and other similar creators will rely on writing completely, but that's not where the application of this skill stops. Writing skills can undoubtedly help you make better ads and make your promotions far more convincing.

Overall, knowing how to write opens up many opportunities for affiliate marketers, and it's really one of the most important cornerstones of affiliate businesses.

## Video Editing

Video editing is another common skill among affiliates who extensively use platforms, such as YouTube, and it is essentially their livelihood. Of course, if you decide to run a blog, for instance, that in no way implies that you shouldn't learn video editing as well. In fact, YouTube is something that many affiliates eventually tap into, even if they worked on different platforms in the past. Videos are simply one of the best ways to engage your audience and make it easier for them to consume your content and, eventually, get acquainted with some of the products and services you are promoting.

## Other Artistic Skills

In essence, almost any artistic skill can be monetized and could make for a very good foundation for an affiliate marketing business. This is why this business is so popular with artists and other creative folks who prefer to freelance and work on their own terms.

You can never learn too much, and your focus should be on expanding your skillset as much as humanly possible throughout your career. You can thus uncover talents you didn't know you possessed or realize that you prefer to do something else with your affiliate career. Drawing, animation, creative writing, and so many other things can immerse your audience and make them care much more about your promotions.

*Nik Neutron*

# Chapter Six: Creating Content

This is where the vast majority of prospective affiliate marketers actually have to begin. Creating content, in the broadest sense you can imagine, is the very foundation that can take some time to build but will allow you to erect an affiliate marketing empire on it if you succeed.

In the previous chapter, you learned how individual platforms operate and how folks can monetize their popularity on them. When it comes to producing quality content, however, the formula for success is a bit more universal, as many of the principles you should adhere to will apply across different ventures, whether you're writing blog posts or making YouTube videos.

In this chapter, we will go over the process of content creation in more depth, and some important advice will be given on how to produce good content and foster a great relationship with your audience. Remember, the healthier and more involved your relationship is with the audience, the greater your affiliate marketing potential will be.

Again, the first step toward producing quality content is finding the right niche. You should spend some time soul searching and asking yourself what it is that you are passionate and knowledgeable about. The lack of knowledge or expertise isn't an insurmountable obstacle, though, as you can teach yourself almost anything in this day and age if you put your mind to it, but passion is something you must have deep inside.

Once you have decided on which niche you will pursue, the next step is to come up with some ideas on how you can use it to provide value and insight to people on the Internet and draw them in. Things like IT, video games, tools, cars, and the like are fairly self-explanatory. With these markets, you will promote either products or well-known services associated with those products, such as repairs, tutorials, and everything else that goes along with that. However, with some niches, it can be more difficult to identify what you as a publisher can offer and what the market demands.

For instance, your interest may lie in philosophy, leading you to start a philosophical blog or YouTube channel, or both. However, what exactly can you write about that to allow you to plug in the products and services that you are promoting? How could people really benefit from this niche? This is the part that you should figure out before starting to plug in the products and services of your partners. Those who care about philosophy specifically could benefit from books on the subject, courses, and similar things. Keep in mind that the most transparent affiliate marketers will also sometimes announce to the audience their plans of becoming affiliates, so it's not out of the question that you can consult with them about what they could be interested in. This can be determined via free surveys or polls, and this can help you take your content in the right direction and ensure that everyone wins.

Niches, such as philosophy, politics, science, and other similar topics, also work well with specific forms of content, such as podcasts. Folks who care about a certain broad topic will want to listen to discussions and thorough analyses for hours in the background while doing their chores and going about their day, and podcasts have become very popular in recent years for this reason.

Other people may not be interested in any concrete information per se, and they could simply be searching online for someone they could look up to or someone who inspires them. This is how many fitness enthusiasts, outdoor explorers, and freethinkers have become popular on various platforms. While these niches may seem a bit vague and not particularly opportune at first glance, this couldn't be further from the truth. Such niches allow you to market all kinds of products, services, tutorials, and much else that could help your audience achieve that which you are doing.

In fact, some affiliate marketers have chosen affiliate marketing itself as their niche. Running a blog or YouTube channel that focuses on affiliate marketing, its many benefits, and how newbies could get in on the business can provide incredible value to those who wish to become affiliates in the future. The more successful you personally are in your niche, the greater your authority will be on the information you provide, and people will listen to what you have to say, which includes your promotions.

Another great way to draw in traffic, particularly if you choose to write a blog or other similar content, is search engine optimization (SEO). This is a useful online tool that many successful affiliate marketers use in order to make their content more relevant and easier to find. In essence, search engine optimization means constructing your articles and other written forms of content in a way that revolves around keywords and specific formats that will help get your blog to the top of the results whenever someone searches for your niche in search engines, such as Google and Bing. SEO is a craft that might take some getting used to, but you can learn the basic formula within hours. After that, it's only a matter of getting creative and improving upon your skills.

Keep in mind that some niches are incredibly saturated on the Internet and can be harder to break into than others. Luckily for you, many content publishers in the most popular niches will just stick to the existing paths and methods and won't provide much in the way of originality. This is why creativity and innovation can give you a significant edge over others. People love to see personality and character, so you shouldn't be afraid to put your own spin on a particular subject, as long as you ensure that your readers or viewers are getting valuable content.

You should also remember what we said about integrity in affiliate marketing. Going for a deal that seems to be the most lucrative on paper may not always be the best idea. Sometimes, even if you see an opportunity to make a quick big buck early on, it may be a good idea to take it slow instead. This is because you should gradually build an intimate relationship with your audience and make it clear to them that your venture isn't all about money. If they see you jumping at every single marketing opportunity, even if it means promoting a substandard or, even worse, irrelevant product, your visitors will quickly become fed up with you. People will come to your blog or channel because you are passionate, informative, inspiring, or funny, not because they want to scroll through a catalog of products, which they can do on Amazon.

If you happen to be using your email list for affiliate marketing as well, you should be especially wary. This means that you will send affiliate links directly to your audience's inbox, and nobody likes spam or uninteresting newsletters. Every now and then, it's a great idea to send a free gift to your subscribers, such as free courses, books, and other products. Better yet, you can strike a deal with your partners to organize a giveaway of something valuable, like a laptop if you are a tech reviewer. Many companies will gladly do this, as it is great marketing for them.

All in all, producing great content is really not a difficult science as long as you put in ingredients like passion, integrity, honesty, and trust — really just the common sense stuff. Even if you are interested in a seemingly obscure niche, you should not despair, as chances are good that there will always be a group of people out there who want to read about it or watch videos on the topic. Artists, political analysts, scientists, engineers, fitness experts, yoga instructors, carpenters, police officers, pet owners, and virtually anyone else can establish an online presence and benefit from affiliate marketing.

*Nik Neutron*

# Chapter Seven: How to Choose Your Niche

For those who are starting out or planning to get started with affiliate marketing, choosing a niche is an essential step in the journey. As we mentioned in the previous chapter, it all starts with cataloging your interests. This is essentially the brainstorming phase of your affiliate business, and you should take your time in considering all the angles, as brainstorming is the very foundation on which every successful business rests.

Furthermore, your decision should take into account the dynamics of the market, and you have to analyze many aspects of a particular niche other than your mere interest in the topic. Unfortunately, we sometimes care deeply about topics that are generally overlooked and uninteresting to most. No matter how much passion you might have for such a niche, you have to be realistic when contemplating its feasibility.

Needless to say, affiliates can expand into a plethora of different niches that correspond with their interests, if they have many. In addition to possibly returning significantly more revenue, such diversification can also help in the way of strategy. That is, experimenting with different niches in affiliate marketing is definitely a good idea because it can allow you to observe your performance in many different fields and, over time, focus on the most successful ones while discarding the rest if they prove burdensome.

Even though some niches are hardly popular and profitable, there are a rare few affiliate marketers who can make it work regardless. With enough inventiveness, originality, and creativity, niches can even be influenced and shaped in a way that draws in an audience. After all, this is how many new trends have started on the Internet in the past. Still, you don't have to perform miracles or invent the wheel to be incredibly successful in affiliate marketing. Further in this chapter, we will take a look at the conventional process of selecting your niche and exploring the things you should consider in greater depth.

## Brainstorming and Entry Strategy

The first step to brainstorming your affiliate marketing plan is to analyze your talents, strengths, weaknesses, and hobbies, as well as to do some research. You can start with a very simple question: asking what your existing hobbies are. If you like drawing in your spare time or discussing politics, you already have some potential ways in right there. You can create your own website or join a platform that lets you publish your art, and once you garner a following, there are plenty of products and services related to this hobby that you can promote. Politics and similar niches, on the other hand, can open up a wide range of opportunities in blogging, video creation, and much more.

People who know how to write, at least on a rudimentary level, have especially good prospects for turning their hobby into an affiliate marketing venture. For instance, engaging in casual carpentry, going hiking, bird-watching, hunting, and countless other hobbies don't really provide opportunities for affiliate marketing in and of themselves. However, if you learn how to piece together some articles, videos, or blog posts, all of these passions can be turned into very successful online businesses. When people enjoy and deeply care about a certain hobby, they also tend to enjoy reading about that hobby and watching related videos online. If you think about it, you will probably realize that you, too, often do the same thing, so there is no reason you shouldn't try to become the one who creates that content yourself.

The more hobbies you have, the better because you'll have a much higher chance of having an easier time breaking into a niche. Finding a niche relevant to your hobby will also prove valuable in the long run because you will likely have to do significantly less research when producing content than someone working in a niche that is foreign to him or her.

In the best-case scenario, if you happen to have significant authority on a given subject, the growth of your platform may come even easier. Many successful affiliate marketers are highly educated individuals who have significant expertise in their niche, which gives them credibility and makes people more likely to view their content. Authority also comes over time to all successful affiliates because of their large audience and good track record. Nonetheless, those with great expertise and experience, whether they are professionals or hobbyists, will certainly have a head start in this regard.

On the off chance that you have no hobbies whatsoever, you shouldn't despair. Many affiliate marketers end up choosing niches that they don't have much experience with. What you should do, however, is make sure that you have at least some interest in your potential niche. Maybe it's some old interest that you never got to involve yourself with or a topic you always wanted to research, but that interest will prove instrumental. Creating content about topics you don't feel connected to on some level can be quite a hassle, and this is something that discourages many affiliate marketers from embarking on this career.

So, after you have listed out your hobbies or interests, the next step is to do some online research to determine a few crucial things. First and foremost, of course, you have to see if your niche of interest is popular. Search for websites, blogs, YouTube channels, and other similar venues for this niche, and pay attention to how much traffic they are drawing and the variety of related products and services that exist on the market. After that, you should look up some of the well-known affiliate programs, which we will cover later in this book, so you can see how much revenue your niche could potentially bring.

You must analyze everything from the feedback that customers give on certain products, which will give you insight into why they prefer certain products and how they use them, as well as the quantity and variety of the said products, which will tell you how wide of a window you have to enter the niche. The broader the niche, the more potential topics and inspiration you will have for your content, as you will also have more choices.

You can take clothing as a great example of this. In and of itself, clothing is a topic so broad that it can hardly be considered a niche in practical terms. However, there are two main advantages to such a niche. For one, clothing is so omnipresent, and it's such a huge part of daily life for many people that successful sales are very likely. Second, there are countless subcategories and numerous angles from which to enter this niche. Most affiliate marketers won't focus on clothing in general but on a specific niche within that field.

If you go too narrow, you might have a hard time finding enough people who are interested, but if you go too wide, you might have similar problems. Of course, your niche must generate enough traffic and interest, but if it's too broad and too competitive, you're in for a struggle. The key is to strike a balance between traffic and competition in just the right way to help you get a foothold and start growing.

So, in our example of the clothing niche, you need to brainstorm and think of a more specific, narrower niche, such as winter clothing, women's dresses, business suits, hiking apparel, and other similar categories. Another example of a broad niche that you'd have to zoom in on could be fishing. In that case, a good niche would be one focusing on fishing rods or catching specific kinds of fish. Examples are countless, but the concept is simple.

Once you've isolated a few potential niches, the next step is to use research and some of the many useful online tools to see how those niches are doing online. The Keyword Planner, made by Google, is one of the keyword research tools that you can use to investigate the search volume of specific keywords that are relevant to your niche. Try to think from the perspective of your audience; put yourself in the position of someone looking for information in your niche, and try to think of the path they'd take to arrive at one of your blogs or websites.

You should identify as many popular keywords as possible, as your content will have to use a combination of multiple keywords to draw in online traffic. These keywords will permeate your content, no matter what platform you might use — blog posts, articles, video descriptions, tags, and many other places are where crucial keywords will be put.

Tools like Quantcast are also very useful in helping you select a niche, especially if you intend to run a website, which most successful affiliates end up doing. Here, you can get all sorts of valuable information about the most popular websites. In particular, if you still don't know what niche you want to go with, you can just use this tool to get a feel for what's popular. As you go further down the list of these big websites, their niches will start getting more and more specific.

More often than not, the most popular websites will deal with a very broad category of content, which is a luxury that only the biggest names in the game have. Your goal is to inspect the most popular categories, and get more specific. Luckily, there are other tools that can help you with that as well. If you're interested in fashion, the idea is to find out which aspects and subcategories of fashion people are interested in, as well as what kind of questions they have.

One of the websites that are very useful for this research is Quora. This is a renowned website that you've probably heard of or even used, where folks come to ask questions and receive multiple answers from competent members of the community. Your only interest will be the questions themselves, and you can search for those by keyword. You can simply type in the wide niche that you're interested in and then explore the inquiries people are making. This is a goldmine of affiliate niche ideas.

# Chapter Eight: How to Know if Your Niche will be Profitable

After you've come up with a list of niches that you're interested in, you should research them further to determine their profitability. Look at other people's blogs and websites, visit forums and see what experienced affiliates have to say about the niche, and pay special attention to the nature of the products and services associated with that niche.

For instance, the role of some products in people's lives is such that they lead to habitual purchases. We all know what those are: basic beauty products, toothpaste, paper towels, and other things we use all the time. The frequency of purchase won't be what makes these products appealing to you because you'll generally make money only once per referral. However, these products are so pervasive that successful affiliates with a lot of traffic can produce many referrals every day, which can add up to a lot despite how cheap the products are and how small the commission is.

On the other hand, some niches provide the opportunity for you to market expensive products that sell far less frequently but yield hefty commissions. Just like the other category, these niches have their pros and cons. It's up to you to decide, based on your business plan and effort you intend to put in, which niche would work best for you. However, there are many other signs to look out for when determining whether or not a niche is profitable.

Internet trends come and go all the time, and they often produce new niches that affiliate marketers can cash in on. Trendy topics and niches are always profitable for someone out there, but being that someone can be difficult. Some affiliates just get lucky with an emerging trend, and by the time that the rest catch on, the competition is already incredibly high. Some niches, however, are seemingly forever popular, and there are always ways to break into the market with enough creativity and planning, and that's always profitable with the right strategy.

It's important to think in the long term, and it's perhaps best to avoid clearly short-lived niches altogether, unless there is a clear opportunity to make quick profit. Some niches include products that are only relevant to certain seasons and, sometimes, even to a one-time phenomenon. For long-term success, you should focus on niches that have been around for a while, with no indication of going out of style in the foreseeable future. As always, there are tools, such as Google Trends, to help you determine the longevity of a niche.

Of course, another simple way to tell if certain niches are profitable is to take a look at some of the many affiliate programs and platforms online. On websites like ClickBank or Amazon's affiliate platform, you can explore countless categories to see exactly how popular they are and how many different products can be marketed in these niches. Just as importantly, you can read about their terms and the commissions these programs offer on different products. Needless to say, commissions are one of the deciding factors in determining the profitability of niches.

These websites also provide you with various tools so that you can sort out the niche products according to different parameters. You will thus see exactly which products sell the most, their average sales, and all sorts of interesting information concerning traffic. The more products and relevant information you see, the more profitable the niche is.

People's common problems are also a source of valuable information that can help identify potentially profitable niches. Some problems that we all have can be rather interesting to write and blog about, and the solutions to these problems might be highly marketable. There are countless such niches in different areas, including health, fitness, diet, and other things that vast numbers of people care about. Most importantly, products and services are abundant, which is putting it mildly.

Those are the general rules of thumb that can help you, but the only way to be truly convinced of a niche's profitability is to thoroughly research that particular niche, and take your time. Feel free to trust your gut feeling to a certain extent as well. On rare occasions, people in all sorts of businesses have seen success, even when going totally against the tide. To help you get an even clearer idea, we will now explore in more detail a few of the most profitable niches, some of which we already mentioned.

## Pets and Pet Products

There are few niches quite as evergreen and profitable as pets and associated products. Not only can all sorts of content be produced about pets in a more general manner, but the niche also has so many sub-categories that it's probably impossible to list them all. Everyone who spends more than half an hour on the Internet will know how much online content revolves exclusively around pets.

If you like animals, especially if you have experience with them, this is one category you have to consider for your niche. Even if you don't want to produce content about dogs, cats, hamsters, and other popular animals, the pet niche can still be incredibly profitable. You can just as easily go with some more exotic, less common niches, like spiders, snakes, or something even more obscure. In fact, this might be even better than pups and kittens because of the great profitability-competition ratio.

On top of that, it's not uncommon for creators to amass a substantial following with content focusing on animals so obscure that you can't even think of them. No matter how unpopular, your animal and pet-oriented niches can still draw attention if done right. People just love animals. Just think of all the products that can be reviewed and marketed in this category.

## Health

Just like pets, health niches are all around us and will likely remain as such until the end of time. If you have any sort of background in health, affiliate marketing in this area can be a solid source of additional income. Many health professionals have their blogs, websites, and YouTube channels where they give valuable advice and information to their audience while promoting a quality product or service here and there.

Beyond professionals, many interesting folks maintain an online following in various alternative medicine niches, which can include anything from marketing products to focusing on overall wellness. As such, health niches focus on much more than just problems. Often, these niches are about healthy living in general or just interesting facts and the science behind all things medicine.

## Fitness

Fitness is an enormous industry nowadays, and it seems like people care about their shape and health more than ever. The scope of products and services pertaining to workouts, cardio, competitions, muscle growth, weight loss, and other similar areas is too vast to even measure.

Vlogging and blogging about one's own fitness regimen have been taking the Internet by storm for a long time, and people are incredibly interested. Many affiliates thus simply document their fitness activities and share that with people online, allowing them to do what they love, remain healthy, and make a living while at it. Supplements, workout gear and equipment, gym programs, courses, diets, and much more are only some of the products and services that can be marketed here.

## Self-Help and Self-Improvement

Self-help, self-improvement, life coaching, and other similar niches have been popular since before the Internet was even a thing. This category generally includes a wide range of niches pertaining to life and life's goals, and many of the niches can overlap with others and come together to form a unique business.

Nowadays, the Internet is crawling with content about dating, meeting career goals, improving confidence, becoming more disciplined, and just changing one's life in general. All of these topics can form individual niches, and each of them can be grown and expanded to be an affiliate's main business. On the other hand, they can also be used separately or molded together into an original life coaching niche. On top of that, self-improvement can certainly apply to many of the niches we mentioned earlier. A workout expert, for instance, can create content focusing on improving one's self physically through exercise while also giving valuable life advice that the audience finds compelling. Many such affiliates already operate on the Internet with millions of faithful followers that they inspire.

## IT

IT is another broad category with a whole lot of niches that millions of affiliates of different interests and backgrounds can benefit from, such as programmers, hardware experts, PC builders, tech enthusiasts, and countless others. A particularly popular and profitable niche is tech review. This niche is insanely competitive, but there's a positive catch in that it's also a niche that can heavily benefit from one's personal touch.

What this means is that, since so many tech reviewers are, more or less, doing the same thing, they have to rely heavily on their own charisma, wit, humor, editing skills, and other similar factors. In theory, this means that anyone who is passionate about technology can break through, and it's a niche where new players are constantly stepping in and making a name for themselves. On top of that, IT is a relatively young market that is in constant, rapid expansion.

# Video Games

Speaking of niches that are expanding and that rely on charisma, video games are all over the Internet, and they seem to keep making gains. When it comes to blogging or running websites, gaming journalism has been rapidly expanding. Just like in the old days when gaming magazines were popular, gaming journalists write about a whole lot of things relevant to video games. These can be reviews, in-depth analyses, essays, the exploration of the technical aspect of video games, and so on. There is a lot of material here for affiliates, and the niche is very accessible to laypersons.

Videos are also an important part of this niche, covering a lot of the things we just mentioned. However, something else that has exploded in recent years is streaming. Players with enough skill and charisma routinely pull in thousands upon thousands of viewers who simply enjoy watching them play on platforms like Twitch. Affiliate marketing opportunities here are abundant. Of course, streaming is popular in niches other than video games as well, but gameplay streams are especially popular.

# Critiques and Reviews

Various forms of reviews, whether written, animated, or recorded, are permeating the Internet across many different markets and niches. Writing quality reviews is a trade that affiliate marketers are strongly advised to master. That is because it works so perfectly with this business.

Affiliate marketing doesn't get much simpler and more direct than writing a review about a product that you like and putting an affiliate link in there. This is how an enormous portion of affiliates make their money, and it works like a charm if done right.

Not only do reviews and various critiques provide valuable information to buyers, but they are also very interesting to read for enthusiasts in various areas. As long as reviews are informative and honest, there are very few limits to how much you can experiment with your format and make your reviews stand out with your personal touch.

# Chapter Nine: Promotional Strategies

When it comes to the actual marketing side of things, it's also worth mentioning that there are two main methods that are employed in affiliate and other forms of marketing. While high- and low-ticket marketing and sales, as we mentioned earlier, are another division, promotional strategies are something else. That is, the aforementioned topic concerns the kind of product you want to promote, while this chapter will focus on the *ways* of promoting that product.

The two main paths to choose from are direct response and indirect marketing. Both of these are solid strategies, but deciding which one is right for you can depend on a lot of factors in the equation. As an affiliate marketer, your ultimate goal is always to sell a product, but you should decide whether you want to sell it by explicitly asking your audience to buy it or if you want to take it slow and get them to arrive at the idea on their own through subtle motivation on your part. This is the difference between direct and indirect marketing.

In direct response marketing, everything revolves around a clear call to action, such as outright asking someone to buy a particular product, which can be done through email, a banner on your blog, an ad on your video, a post on your social media, and other similar methods. Direct marketing is also usually aimed at a very specific group of individuals who are deemed to be potential buyers of a certain product or service. When you, as a regular user on the Internet, visit a certain blog, for example, and you see an advert telling you to buy something for a certain reason, that's direct marketing.

There doesn't have to be a reason stated, though, because it's often assumed that you're interested based on the content you're viewing at that time. For instance, if you write a blog post about the best ways to go about getting rid of moles in one's garden and then put an ad that urges visitors to buy your gardening e-book in the sidebar, that's a direct and reasonable form of marketing. The same applies to email calls to action, which are usually based on where a certain user subscribed and gave his or her address. If a user provides his or her email address on a page that offers a particular online course, then affiliate marketers who run that page will often subsequently send that user emails about other courses and similar offers.

As you can see, direct response marketing is tailored and precise, and, if you are wise, it's used only with good prospects, where you are almost certain that sales will occur. Marketers arrive at this conclusion based on a thorough analysis and priming of their potential customers whose behavior and wishes they are well-acquainted with.

You can also probably see some potential downsides to direct marketing. That is, direct marketing runs the risk of being the most annoying to Internet users, and it's the main reason why some people avoid giving out their email addresses or use ad-blocking extensions on their browsers. Thus, clever affiliate marketers need to be very careful not to push their audience too far and lose credibility. After all, you don't want to gamble with your platform and push people away by engaging in spam, whether it's actually spam or just perceived as such.

On the other hand, indirect marketing is much more subtle, strategic, and oriented toward the long term. This form of marketing puts a strong emphasis on customer engagement and providing value to the audience so as to make them genuinely interested in a product or service. In essence, it is everything we talked about thus far — the careful content creation, the platform building, and the strengthening of the bond between publisher and audience; all of these are, in a way, indirect affiliate marketing.

There are many clear benefits to this approach, including trust, interest, and even support from your audience and potential customers. When they see you providing valuable content for them and showing genuine care for their best interests, your visitors will want to engage with the things you promote, and, if they are aware of how businesses like yours work, they will also want to help you make money through your marketing efforts. After all, that revenue is what's keeping their favorite content creators above water. Thus, in the simplest terms, indirect marketing is, above all, the presentation and introduction of products and services, as opposed to a specific call to action.

Not everything about indirect marketing is perfect, though. For one, it's not very analytics-friendly, which means that success rates pertaining to sales that resulted from indirect marketing efforts can be difficult to ascertain. Of course, producing content and engaging with a large audience regularly can take a lot of time and effort. However, this isn't exactly a problem if you are a content creator who enjoys your work and who is passionate about your niche, as we discussed earlier.

Taking the benefits and shortcomings into account, it's clear that the best affiliate marketing strategy will make use of both of these promotional strategies. After all, once you consider all the factors and how the market functions, you will realize that it's only natural to use both direct and indirect marketing. If you spend time providing content to your followers, as well as take the time to promote products to them transparently and in detail, it's completely normal to subsequently use calls to action to get them to buy the said products. As such, a thorough affiliate marketing campaign will use indirect forms of marketing first to prepare and groom potential customers for sales and then round everything up with a call to action, thus producing maximum results.

This way, you will never have to resort to spamming, using ad saturation, or annoying your followers in any way. Everything you market to them directly will be a logical and relevant result of what they have been reading or watching from you up to that point. As you can see, indirect affiliate marketing is essentially the entire professional life of a content creator who uses affiliate marketing to make a living off of that which he or she loves.

# Chapter Ten: How to Promote Your Affiliate Offers

Now that you understand the technical basics of affiliate promotion, you will be able to get to work creating quality content that draws in traffic. The content you create will be your bread and butter – the central pillar of success in this business. In this chapter, we'll go through some simple tips on how to optimize your content and do a better job of promoting your affiliate products and your platform.

First and foremost, you must remember and adhere to one golden rule of affiliate marketing. It's simple: your affiliate programs should be chosen in accordance with the content you are making, as opposed to adjusting and changing your content to accommodate those programs. This means that your content should dictate what you'll promote, and your quality, transparency, honesty, and audience's favorite format should not be compromised.

Of course, you will make use of keywords and make some minor accommodations if you are trying to plug an affiliate product in seamlessly, but the fundamental aspects of your platform, which are what draws an audience in the first place, should be cherished. The career of sellouts and greedy folks who don't care about their content or audience usually meets an untimely demise sooner rather than later.

Therefore, you should value your audience's feedback on everything you do. Successful affiliate marketers understand this, which is why they sometimes hire help to assist them in keeping track of feedback if the audience is too big for one person to handle. If your audience criticizes you for promoting a certain product in a way they don't appreciate, you have to pay heed to that and do better next time.

If your audience is generally okay with the way you promote things, then you should engage them as directly as possible. Remember to collect email addresses whenever you can, and build your email list because this is a great way of promoting affiliate products directly to your most loyal followers who are, of course, most likely to buy based on your recommendation in the first place.

Another good way of promotion is through collaborations with other affiliate marketers whose business is on a similar level. This is especially popular among content creators whose business is more visual, such as YouTube creators. The underlying principle is simple: you get in touch with another creator whose niche is different but related and connected in some way to yours, and you create a piece of content together. This allows both of you to pull in some extra viewers from each other's audiences. On top of that, affiliate links and various other offers can be shared on both of your platforms to generate even more conversions.

This type of deal would work best between creators whose niches feed into or complement each other. For instance, say you are running a YouTube channel focusing on video games, but you know some other creator who publishes art and fan fiction related to those games. This is a good opportunity for collaboration because there is likely to be a significant crossover between the two of you when it comes to your audiences' interests.

Something else to keep in mind is that platforms like YouTube have intricate algorithms that determine which videos get recommended and who turns up on top. Just like Google's search engine results, this system bases those results on certain parameters. On YouTube and many other sites and networks, consistency is very important. The release of your content should ideally be a thing of schedule and, of course, as frequent as possible. Content creators that focus on these things will generally grow faster than those who publish thrice a week and then take a break for a month, after which they publish just one piece of content.

Most importantly, whatever platform or search engine your traffic depends on, you must research and acquaint yourself thoroughly with those algorithms to take full advantage of them. Learn the ins and outs of SEO, and study the way search engines like Google and Bing work. Your success depends on it.

As we mentioned earlier, your main niche should be one that lasts, but that doesn't mean you shouldn't try to take advantage of important seasons and arising trends. These can be great opportunities to expand your audience and sell more products than usual through various specials that your niche might allow for. Once you get to a certain point, you will also be able to afford doing giveaways, which people love. A popular way of doing this is to ask your followers to do certain things as a means of gaining entry into the giveaway. These are almost always free and easy actions for your fans, such as sharing your post on social media, subscribing to your email newsletter, and many other things that can be incredibly helpful for your growth.

In the end, it's all about paying close attention to what works for others, adapting that in a creative and personalized manner, and observing how your audience behaves and reacts. Through attentiveness and use of many tools and resources on the Internet, you should get a good hang of it in time.

# Chapter Eleven: The Top Affiliate Marketing Programs or Networks

Affiliate marketing programs or platforms comprise the fourth pillar of affiliate marketing that we briefly went over in the first chapter. Depending on the individual network, this party's role in the process can focus on just bringing affiliates and brands together, or it can be much more intimately involved. For instance, major affiliate networks, such as Amazon Associates or Commission Junction, will also take care of your payments, provide you with detailed financial reports and statistics, and just generally run a portion of your affiliate business for you, as well as help you grow. More often than not, these networks are something that an already established content creator will join in order to consolidate his or her affiliate business and make it more professional and efficient. Once you've started raking in serious money through one of these platforms, you will have reached new heights in your business venture.

In this chapter, we will take a look at some of the most established affiliate networks, how they can help affiliates, and how you can join them if you feel that you could profit from their services.

## Amazon Associates

With the countless articles that it sells, Amazon has a platform that offers an incredible opportunity for all affiliate marketers. In addition to being one of the largest, Amazon Associates is also a very old platform that has been around for a long time in the affiliate marketing industry.

Joining the network is very easy, and, most importantly, it is free. After you join, the process of marketing will be a piece of cake. Essentially, all you have to do is choose some of the countless products being sold on Amazon, get the website to generate an affiliate link, and then plug that unique link into your blog, video description, website content, or anywhere else that you can. Write a review about a television set, include an Amazon affiliate link, and wait for commissions to begin trickling in.

On Amazon, you will also find a detailed table of commissions, so you can see exactly how much money you'd be making from promoting specific product categories. Amazon isn't exactly known for shockingly high commission rates, but if you're generating traffic and promoting a popular, quality product, you can acquire serious profits.


## ClickBank

Also around for quite a while, specifically about 20 years, ClickBank is another major platform with an affiliate program that many use with success. As a retailer, ClickBank mostly focuses on digital products, including but not limited to software and e-books, but physical products are also on offer.

Just like the Amazon Associates program, ClickBank will provide you with affiliate links, but it's also known for some rather high commissions with particular products. What also helped build up ClickBank's reputation includes its reliable and secure payments and thorough analytics. This program is a good network for those affiliates who want to keep a detailed track of their marketing success and improve their strategies based on such results. It's also free to sign up to this network.

## Commission Junction (CJ Affiliate)

Formerly known as Commission Junction, CJ Affiliate is yet another major venue for vendors and affiliates, which is free and accessible to join. It's a well-established network that's easy to navigate and get used to, with a great range of commissions that can go to considerable heights.

Just like most other affiliate programs, all you need is a developed online platform where you can advertise products, and you are likely to be admitted to the network. CJ Affiliate is also popular among those who wish to monetize their mobile apps.

This network also offers special status to the most successful affiliates, who are viewed as premier publishers because of the high amount of traffic they get. This is their CJ Performer Program, and it can help successful affiliates rake in thousands upon thousands of dollars in commissions every month.

## ShareASale

Although it's a bit younger than some of the networks we mentioned, ShareASale has built quite a strong reputation for itself. In addition to being trusted by experienced affiliates, thanks to its transparency and honesty, the network is also rather versatile and diversified. Affiliates from all sorts of backgrounds can approach this network, and chances are good that they will find products and services that are just right for them and their niche.

Like ClickBank and many other networks, ShareASale deals in performance-based advertising, so statistics and analytics are strongly emphasized. As an affiliate, you will be able to track your performance thoroughly and remain up to speed at all times. Those who are already into affiliate marketing but are doing it through a more niche network can greatly benefit from ShareASale's program if they want to diversify.


## JVZoo

JVZoo focuses largely on digital products, including product launches. This is one of the fastest-growing companies in the business, and they can provide some hefty commissions to affiliates at times. It isn't unheard of to score a thousand dollars per sale with some of the more expensive products or launches. JVZoo is also considered an SaaS, or software as a service.

Like the others, JVZoo helps you keep an eye on your analytics and will also notify you of each sale, if you so desire. What's also great about JVZoo is just how friendly the site is to beginning affiliate marketers. Thanks to its training programs and tools that help teach new affiliates the ropes, this is a great platform for those who want to learn the affiliate business and begin making money as soon as they get the hang of it. As always, all you really need is a followership to monetize.

## MaxBounty

While MaxBounty is another network that brings together both affiliates and vendors, the network makes it no secret that their emphasis is on the affiliates and their success. This is a network that focuses on the cost per action model in a very broad sense. Not only can you, as the affiliate, make money per sale, but you can also partner up with someone who just wants traffic. As such, affiliates on MaxBounty can earn money from driving their audience to sign up to websites, subscribe with their emails, and much more.

Keep in mind that many of these networks, such as JVZoo, for example, will ensure that they also provide opportunities for recurring commissions, and some might put a strong emphasis on this model, making it their priority. If you want to focus on one type of commission more than the others, then you should seek out the networks that are best suited for that. There are dozens of enormous affiliate networks out there, apart from the ones we just mentioned here, and the smaller ones are probably in the thousands. All told, unless you have the luck to be approached by a huge individual brand or vendor for a lucrative affiliate deal, joining a reputable network is your best bet at success.

*Nik Neutron*

# Chapter Twelve: Pros of Affiliate Marketing

While we already mentioned quite a few benefits of affiliate marketing, there are some more pros that should be outlined. We will also cover some downsides of this endeavor in the next chapter so that you can weigh the pros and cons against each other. As a prospective affiliate marketer, you will know best what you are getting into once you are fully appreciative of both sides of the coin.

## Personal Autonomy

Right off the bat, one of the most frequently cited pros of affiliate marketing is the fact that it will give you autonomy and a kind of freedom that hardly comes by with a nine-to-five cubicle job. This is why many folks embark on this journey in the first place. However, the important thing is to understand that freedom does not mean doing no work. As you have learned thus far, plenty of work can go into building a successful affiliate marketing business, depending on your situation and aspirations.

The beauty of this is that affiliate marketing is a tool that lets you draw in revenue while doing something you love — and doing it for yourself. For most people, doing something they love is the very meaning of freedom, no matter how much work it entails. As such, affiliate marketing is one of the best ways to unburden yourself of bosses, the office, the cubicle, the dreaded nine-to-five routine, and many other things that you might feel are smothering you right now.

## Growth Potential

Your personal growth and prospects in this business aside, affiliate marketing is something that is growing exponentially as an industry. As the Internet grows, the copious amounts of online content that people consume every day rapidly boost the utility of affiliate marketing.

As things stand right now, the majority of publishers online utilize affiliate marketing programs and deals to make money off of their work and Internet platforms. In fact, affiliate marketing has already become a multi-billion-dollar industry a couple of years ago, and it is only expected to grow in the near future. In less than two years, affiliate marketing is expected to grow to around seven billion dollars. Of course, it's always a great thing when the industry you want to enter is growing, so now is as good of a time as any to get in on this business.

## An Agreeable Business

Versatility is another great perk that affiliate marketers can benefit from. That is, affiliate marketing is a source of income that is applicable to a wide range of creative and publishing endeavors. This also means that it's a business that is very easy to work with, so to speak. Affiliate marketers can strategize, improvise, and take many liberties with how they will structure their affiliate business because there are few rules when it comes to how you can do it and with what kind of intensity.

This opens up opportunities for a whole lot of people from different backgrounds and interests. Whether you run a website, publish paintings, create videos, make courses, or write articles, affiliate marketing is likely to be suitable as a source of additional income. You've learned just how easy it is once you have a platform, so even if you are pulling in a decent income through other means, affiliate marketing can send even more revenue your way with minimal effort.

## High Personal Ceiling

It's not just that affiliate marketing is an industry in expansion. This is a business where the limit of how much you can grow and prosper is set very high. The success of your affiliate marketing venture is generally proportionate to how much you grow and develop your publishing platform. The bigger your following becomes, the more sales you will be able to facilitate.

This also means that you have the liberty to set your own limits. In case you want affiliate marketing to become a source of additional income on the side, for instance, you can deliberately grow the business only to a certain point. That will entail less engagement and commitment, allowing you to focus on other things while still complementing your revenue stream. On the other hand, you are free to build your affiliate marketing business to incredible heights. On top of that, there are no limits to the platforms and programs you can utilize, which means that affiliate marketers can expand across multiple platforms and use them in unison for maximum reach and efficiency.

## Schedule Flexibility and Time Management

Needless to say, working from home has many benefits, which some people will find more important than others. At any rate, it's undeniable that this sort of arrangement affords one some rather convenient, objective perks, one of which is the ability to set your own time.

Even though, like we discussed, affiliate marketing can entail plenty of work, the ability to modify one's schedule is something that certain people will benefit from immensely. It's true that some folks thrive on the rigid structures and schedules provided to them by others, but some like to organize their own days. The truth is that traditional arrangements can sometimes hinder an employee's performance. For instance, it has been proven through research that early birds and night owls are more than conceptions of popular culture. Some folks are truly more efficient and comfortable when working at night, but most jobs rarely allow that. Affiliate marketing lets you make your own hours, decide when you want to engage in leisure, and lets you go on vacation when you please, as long as your breaks are organized in a way that won't hurt your revenue. Either way, you'll be the one calling the shots.

## Low Investment – High Potential Return

It should be reiterated that low entry costs comprise one of the most important benefits of affiliate marketing, and this is what draws so many people in. Joining most affiliate programs is free. You can find lots of useful advice, and guidance is free. Promoting your content and growing your online following can also be completely free with the right strategy.

Coupled with the potential to make serious bank in the long term, this makes affiliate marketing a rather low-investment, low-risk venture. Most kinds of failure in this business don't really bring about any serious consequences either, in the sense that you are unlikely to lose much of what you've had before starting out as an affiliate.

Needless to say, working from home has immense financial benefits, regardless of what your job is. Depending on your lifestyle and other activities apart from work, your transportation costs are likely to be significantly cut. You will also possibly spend less money on food if you used to eat at restaurants during your lunch breaks at work. A freelancer's main expenses are bills, of course, and any investment that they want to put into their business. These investments are highly adjustable in affiliate marketing, ranging from virtually no investment to certain expenses that you might incur if you decide to create websites and the like.

## Never Mind Customer Service

As an affiliate marketer, your job will de facto consist of selling things to customers, but the nature of the business is such that you will have next to nothing to do with said customers. This is quite a convenient arrangement because most other jobs that revolve around sales will entail some form of customer service or feedback, particularly when sales turn sour for the buyer. In our case, this is the job of the merchant, as the merchant is the one most responsible for quality control, shipping, and subsequent support.

All you have to do is try your best to evaluate products beforehand, and ensure that you are promoting useful items or services merely for your reputation and credibility in the eyes of your audience. If a shipment goes badly, for instance, it won't be your fault, and the vast majority of people will understand that perfectly well. Besides, affiliate marketers always have the luxury of explaining the situation to their loyal audience and distancing themselves from brands and sellers that mess up.

## Community

Indeed, there is also a community aspect to affiliate marketing, so to speak. Given that affiliate marketers are Internet-savvy folks with a constant presence in cyberspace, there are many forums and online communities where they congregate. Of course, these communities are highly accessible and easy to interact with, which has all sorts of perks.

For once, you will be able to seek valuable advice from those with experience and learn a lot from what they have done with their business. You will be able to learn about people's individual experiences with particular affiliate programs and whether or not these programs are good for your exact plans and aspirations. Various forms of collaboration are always a possibility, and they happen frequently between publishers. Sometimes, the potential revenue can be good enough for two publishers to collaborate on a project and later share the profit from commissions.

## Legal and Technical Benefits

Some of the perks of affiliate marketing are beyond just the business itself. In the United States, for instance, affiliate marketers and other freelancers are usually, in effect, running and owning a business, which means that you would be entitled to certain benefits. In this racket, there is always a possibility that you will need a new computer, tablet, another gadget, or some other relevant resource. These business expenses can be used to write off some taxes.

All told, after you get to a certain point, and your affiliate marketing venture reaches a certain level of organization and profitability, you will essentially be a business owner.

Furthermore, unlike in some other marketing rackets, affiliates generally don't have to worry about the technical aspect of advertising, such as the creation of banners and other promotional materials. This job will rest with the merchant and their marketing teams. All you have to do is generate interest, drive traffic, and hopefully convert that into sales. Moreover, as a publisher and affiliate who promotes relevant products, your content itself is what already produces interest.

## Passive Income

Of course, passive income is one of the most renowned benefits of affiliate marketing. It is the dream – the crowning achievement of a successful affiliate business that makes it all worth it. Once you are sufficiently adept and successful, a growing portion of your income will likely start to take the form of passive revenue. Affiliates who have grown their audience to a great size, successfully promoted all the right products, and established a strong feeling of trust with their audience will find it incredibly easy to generate sales.

After a while, all it might take is to create a quality piece of content and slap an affiliate link somewhere visible. Your viewers or readers will flock to check out the product, and many of them will start purchasing, thus transferring money to you via the commissions in the process. All you have to do after that is get up in the morning, scroll through your numbers, and eventually collect.

# Chapter Thirteen: Cons of Affiliate Marketing

Anyone who is considering getting into affiliate marketing, or any other venture for that matter, should also be acquainted with the negative aspects, of course. As you have seen thus far, the pros and benefits of affiliate marketing are plentiful, but nothing in life is really perfect. Thus, there are certainly a few cons to this whole racket, which we will cover in this chapter to help you see the full picture and make the most informed decisions later on.

## Conditions Set by the Merchant

Perhaps the first con of affiliate marketing that should be mentioned is one aspect of the nature of this whole arrangement. That is, affiliates are the ones who have to connect with merchants or sign up for affiliate programs, which are designed and structured in a way that the vendor sees fit. Of course, that means you will be operating in accordance with someone else's rules and are subject to their terms.

While it's true that individual merchants can be negotiated with to adjust certain parameters of your arrangement with them, there is no guarantee that they will comply. Moreover, when it comes to major affiliate programs, those are generally non-negotiable. Circumstances can change, and terms that used to be adequate can begin to divert from your newly arising interests, but chances are good that you won't be able to change anything. You certainly have the liberty to choose who you want to work with and quit the program, but those will often be your only options, which is definitely a disadvantage.

## Competitive Niches

Even though they might be interesting and highly appealing to you, some niches on the Internet are just incredibly competitive nowadays. This is usually due to the saturation of content creators who are already hard at work and doing a good job for millions of people. Such niches can be rather difficult to break into, so this is a con that many fresh affiliate marketers end up facing.

The biggest problems arise when such niches are the only ones you can or want to do. Needless to say, this can discourage folks and make them feel like affiliate marketing is not for them and that they just can't do it. Of course, if you think you can't do it, then you're probably right, and vice versa. The trick to breaking into such niches is a solid, detailed plan and perseverance. On top of that, creativity and originality go a long way. No niche is actually impossible to get into, but some will require you to apply yourself more than others — that much is true.

## Time Management

Indeed, we did list the freedom to do your own time management as an advantage, but it can also definitely be a disadvantage in some cases. For the part of the population that prefers it when others provide them with a schedule and daily assignments, being in charge of their own time can pose a problem. That is, being truly in charge of your day is sometimes more difficult than it sounds.

As counterintuitive as it might seem, freedom and autonomy come with plenty of responsibilities. Affiliate marketers must know how to organize themselves and make sure that they neither overwork themselves nor start slacking. This is an issue for many other freelancers who work from home, not just those in affiliate marketing. As such, some affiliate marketing ventures will require you to know and be in control of yourself to a great extent. Artists, video makers, and other similar creators will ultimately have to organize their own projects and set their own deadlines, which are more difficult than they might seem at first.

## Risking Your Platform

If you are a successful publisher or content creator who has a well-built platform with many followers, but you also happen to be shortsighted, you might end up putting everything you've worked for at risk. This is why it's important to enter this business without any preconceptions of making a quick buck and having an easy time.

There are plenty of ill-informed publishers who view affiliate marketing as an easy cash grab, so they resort to spam, low-quality promotion, and just overall saturation. Sometimes, this might work for a while, which can make matters even worse because these affiliates will also start to focus on producing much more content than they used to so they can put up as many ads and promotions as possible. As always, a focus on quantity tends to degrade the quality, and this can completely ruin your platform. Combining greedy marketing tactics with a decrease in the quality of your content, all for the sake of output, is an excellent path toward disaster. As such, affiliate marketers need to be careful and think in the long term, which can sometimes mean turning down deals and avoiding programs that might seem appealing in the short term.

## The Commissions

The commission-based income itself can perhaps be viewed as a con. On the most fundamental level, no income in affiliate marketing can be guaranteed. Success-oriented affiliates don't concern themselves with this, but it is technically possible to put in a lot of work and come up with next to nothing in the way of revenue. This should virtually never happen with the right strategy and effort, but the nature of the business is such that this must be outlined as a potential con.

That is, because your income is not predetermined or fixed in any way and is completely based on your performance and ability to generate certain actions from your audience, it's difficult to predict your income. This should in no way suppress your ambitions of becoming a successful affiliate marketer, but you should always be prepared for occasional disappointments just in case. Luckily, this whole issue works both ways, and it's also what gives affiliate marketing such a high potential profitability. Such is the nature of performance-based income: you can earn anywhere between pocket change to potential millions.

# Technical Vulnerabilities and Scams

Perhaps this is true with most online businesses, but it's also a noteworthy con with affiliate marketing. Doing virtually anything on the Internet will always leave you somewhat vulnerable to certain security risks to some degree. Most folks get by just fine, and they don't encounter any major problems, but caution is always advised.

There will always be folks out there looking to scam others and cash in on someone else's work, so affiliate marketers need to be careful who they partner up with. This is also where the aforementioned community aspect is quite beneficial, as you can always research what other affiliates think of certain merchants and determine whether they are reputable.

The hijacking of affiliate links is also not unheard of. Savvy scammers can sometimes hijack these links and direct the commissions from any sales to them instead of the affiliate who was given that link. Small-time affiliates might not even notice that something is wrong, and they might attribute the lack of income to their own poor performance. On the flipside, these hackers and Internet thieves will seldom feel that attacking beginning affiliates is profitable, so the risk is very low, but it's there.

# The Merchant's Additional Powers

Apart from setting the terms, commissions, and other important aspects of the program, the merchants also have a hold over their affiliates in that they could potentially damage their reputation at times.

When you're just starting out, it's best to go with very reputable vendors who are known for quality products, excellent customer service, and reliable shipping. Your first affiliate gigs should be smooth and result in as many satisfied members of your audience as possible. As your career progresses and you acquire more loyal followers, you will have some room for the occasional mistake of promoting the wrong company or product. However, you don't want your first promotions to be disastrous and establish you as someone who promotes bad products because this reputation can be difficult to reverse.

Caution and research are the name of the game. You should always do your due diligence and look through all the points and terms of a particular affiliate program. There could be all sorts of additional unspoken aspects of the deal that you might disagree with.

## The Lifestyle

While it can liberate you from a job you hate and provide you with great professional opportunities, the freelance lifestyle certainly has its downsides. However, the thing is that these downsides can also be advantages, depending on a person's disposition.

For one, some can see working from home as being an isolating experience. In fact, it's undeniable that some folks love the office environment and thrive in it, so they would miss it dearly if they started to work from home. Luckily, there are things like co-working public spaces and libraries where you can not only be among random people but possibly work together with other freelancers who might even be doing the same exact job as you. Of course, if all you want is to be outside, you can always take your work with you to a café or anywhere else you find comfortable. You will need little more than your phone and laptop.

Loneliness is not the only issue, though. Working from home can lead to a very sedentary lifestyle, which can have implications on your health if you don't compensate with some exercise. With enough organization and a solid schedule, though, all of these issues can be solved.

## Constant Need for New Buyers

In many forms of affiliate marketing, a conversion or commission will be a one-time thing. That is, after you refer a new customer to a particular vendor through your link, it will be difficult to make more commissions off of that particular person in the future. They might end up coming back to the store to buy more products, but those won't be your referrals. It's possible to make multiple commissions from one buyer if you market individual products, but if they really like the vendor you introduced them to, they will just go to them directly in the future instead of through your links each time.

This is why the already-discussed differences between low-ticket, high-ticket, and recurring affiliate marketing are so important. Those products and services that come with a recurring program are the only ones guaranteed to bring in commissions from the same person over an extended period. You refer the customer once to subscribe or enroll, and each new payment yields a commission. Otherwise, affiliate marketing is all about the constant generation of new, fresh traffic. In essence, that means that building a base of customers is generally difficult, unlike in other sales businesses.

*Nik Neutron*

# Chapter Fourteen: Growing an Email List

So far, you have learned what affiliate marketing is, what its benefits and pros and cons are, as well as how you can become a successful marketer, find your right niche, and approach brands. You pretty much know how to get started. Now, it is time to delve deep and expand your business as an affiliate marketer. From this chapter onwards, you will learn the nitty-gritty of expanding your affiliate marketing business.

The number one priority when building an online business is building an email list. Imagine that 20% of all your work brings 80% of the profits like the 80/20 principle. Building an email list is similar to 80% benefits. Any successful entrepreneur will advise you that mistakes are a part of the learning process. However, if there is one thing they can go back in time and do, it would be to start building an email list sooner. Once your website has been created and set up, start by collecting emails by offering forms to the visitors to sign up.

The email list is a business's most important asset as it is the prime connection to their subscribers. It is about maintaining direct relationships. If there are 50,000 people who subscribe to your website and they are not concerned about your company or your product then your list might not be worth it. Even worse, it may cost you money. A monthly fee would be taken by your service provider based on the number of subscribers. Therefore, the actual assets of the company are the ones who are engaged with the products. They are the people who are interested in purchasing your product or services. You have to focus on building a list of quality subscribers rather than the merely focusing on the quantity. What matters is how you maintain a good relationship with your subscribers. Many marketers might disagree, saying it's safer to have a list with a large number of subscribers. However, a smaller list of quality subscribers who engage with the website is better than a big list of mostly uninterested customers.

## Importance of growing your email list:

Here are several reasons why it is important to have an email list:

1. Your Facebook, Instagram, or Twitter followers might be thousands in number, but since these platforms do not belong to you, you have no control over your main assets. If one of these platforms were to shut down one day, all your connections to your customers are lost. If you have a website that belongs to you, the email list belongs to you automatically. However, you must keep your list backed up regularly. An Excel document or a cloud storage service, such as Dropbox, can be used for storage. They might just be a list of emails but it is worth more than you know.

2. Email is a direct connection to your target audience. It can help in building rapport and maintaining relationships with them. An effective way to understand the needs, desires, and pains of your audience is by surveying them through email. Engaging in a conversation with your subscribers can always help you in finding out which product or

service needs to be focused on. This can also let them be aware of your product. Features like notifications on the publication of new articles and promotions will encourage them to visit your website more often.

3. It is the most cost effective and beneficial way to provide true value to customers who are interested. Emails are a free channel for promoting products to an audience that is already into your business. It is a free means of product promotion and has the highest conversion rate when compared to any other promotional channel. Therefore, building a list of engaged subscribers will always help you build a much stronger and profitable business.

4. An email list can help create partnerships within the industry. It will be easier because you have the exposure to your audience to offer. You will be well appreciated in your field if you can help gain visibility towards an interesting market.

## How to grow your email list

The process of gathering email addresses is effortless. All it requires is an option where the visitors of your website can give their information, like name, email address, etc., and a marketing service to collect, store, and arrange the information. Generally, people are not so keen on giving away their personal information. It is your responsibility to convince them through the website that the information is given for a good reason. A free gift can be offered in exchange for their information. This practice is called a lead magnet. Let's explore this in detail.

Your first task would be to find the right system to organize these emails. An email marketing system will collect, store, organize, and create automated messages. They can also be used to split test and track campaign information. These services are mostly charged on a monthly basis or will depend on the number of subscribers. The cost will be increased as the number increases. When choosing an email management provider, certain conditions should be examined.

## Automation:

A feature that automates messages according to a given date and time is very important.

## Segmentation:

When you can segment subscribers based on preferences and interests, it improves the efficiency of your campaigns. For instance, you can separate people who have subscribed and received a free gift from the people who signed up for more services. Therefore, you can manage different campaigns for each segment based on their preferences.

## A/B testing:

This feature is vital to improving your marketing strategies for a successful business. A/B testing can help send one type of email (A) to half of your audience and another type of email (B) to the other half. You can observe which type has the best results. You can see the percentage of subscribers who opened the mail or clicked a link in the mail. The difference between the two types will be the subject line, the text, the product, etc. Testing helps you optimize the way your campaign functions and benefits your business. Here are three recommended email marketing services you can start out with:

i) AWeber.com: This is quite an affordable option and also a complete management system. Its elements are automation, tracking, and subscriber segmentation. It has a simple interface and provides customer care support every day. Their website includes video tutorials that explain the different features it has. You will have access to all the features, regardless of the plan you choose. For up to 500 subscribers, $19 is the monthly fee (at the time this book is being written).

ii) MailChimp.com: This is a very popular and simple email marketing service. They include a free plan for up to 2000 subscribers, which is a good place to start for beginners. This free plan only includes a few of the basic features required. You can upgrade as your budget increases. It is convenient as it will allow you to collect email addresses right after you install it. The paid plan gives you access to A/B testing, full data campaigns, which are all, required to run a successful campaign. The service also provides you with video tutorials on how to use their features. It also comes with live customer support, but it's available only for the paid plan.

iii) GetResponse.com: The basic plan is $15 per month, and it gives you access to all the features required to start a business. The user interface is quite simple to get around, whereas the video tutorials are easy to understand. It includes 24/7 customer care live chat and assistance over email or phone. The sign-up forms and landing pages they provide are quite appealing. With an extra $15, you will have access to unlimited landing pages.

## The lead magnet

You have definitely come across forms that state, "subscribe to our newsletter," on several websites. You would probably not be bothered by it unless the website has to provide information that you don't want to miss out on. On the other hand, if they were to provide you with a free gift of high value, you would give away your email address. For this particular gift to be considered important, it has to be something that your customers need. If you have done the proper research required, then you already know what your audience prefers. This gift should be something that is a solution to the issues similar to solution your paid product provides. This high-value offer should not be expensive or time-consuming to prepare. It just has to solve the problem.

For instance, a fitness instructor is selling an online program for men who want to increase their muscle mass. The free gift should be a cheat sheet that provides a sneak peek into what the website will provide. This information will land an email address for sure. To see this cheat sheet as having an increased value, it has to be a well-designed PDF, with images of exercise.

Therefore, a lead magnet can be different things:

- An eBook

- An audio file

- A video tutorial

- A short course

- A cheat sheet

- A free live video consultation

These freebies can be delivered at your doorstep or through an email address, for instance, a short video course in three parts. This approach is practical because it builds a connection with the subscribers. They will look forward to the next video in the series and will get used to your emails in their inbox. One important factor is that the freebie should be relevant to the product that you're selling. Your subscribers are only great if they become potential buyers or brand advocates.

In the last example provided, the trainer gives a cheat sheet as a freebie and the paid product was the online fitness programs. Let's say the trainer gave away a video game as the incentive. This is obviously not relevant to the product. There is no reason to convince yourself that the person opting for the video game would purchase the fitness program. It is because the two programs are not related.

## The sign-up form

The sign-up form is the actual form that the visitors to the website use to enter their name and email address. It can be placed in strategic locations to optimize the number of people who sign up. Your marketing service would provide several templates that would be easy to customize and edit. You have to choose a form that matches your brand and looks professional.

The headline to your form should state the service you provide and a solution. It should also mention what they would receive as a result of signing up. It's always a good idea to lay it out in bullet points. For instance, a heading may say, "five easy exercises for the upper body." Then, the details, such as its benefits, should be provided in a short message format that should be easily understood at a glance. Make sure to use the right font size and colors that suit your brand design. It should also stand out on the website.

There will be a call-to-action button on the form that plays a vital role. It mostly contains instructions to a visitor on what to do next. It is better to use words other than "subscribe," and choose a more beneficial verb. "Download now" or "get access now" are some examples that have been proven to give good results. Moreover, make sure that the button stands out, so give it a contrasting color to attract attention.

The placement of the sign-up form on the web page can make a big difference in conversion. Your website must be designed to achieve the maximum number of email lists. For this, there are places in which the forms, when positioned, can increase the chance of the visitors turning into subscribers.

## *Above the fold:*

This is the portion where the visitor arrives on your site, even before navigating it. Use a feature box that fills up the entire screen. This helps convert all the visitors into subscribers very easily as long as the free gift is exciting enough.

### The upper right sidebar:

This is one of the most common places to add it.

### Above the top menu:

Within WordPress, there is a free plugin called "Hello Bar" that gives a thin horizontal form above the web page's top navigation menu.

### After each blog post:

Once a person has read one of your articles to the end, he or she has just demonstrated an interest in your content. This is the kind of person who forms your audience base, and you would want this person to join the mailing list. Therefore, you have to place the form right after the post. If you offer a freebie, you will get a better result. It could be an action plan or a checklist that compliments your article. For example, if the article is about content marketing, a freebie could be five interesting headline templates.

### At the beginning of each post:

If you write long articles, there is a possibility where you can give an option to download it as a PDF version, which they can print or save for later. It's always considered to be a safe tactic that works wonders. The reader would then enter the email address to download it.

Pop-up forms: This can be a bit annoying most of the time, but somehow, it always gets good results. After using pop-up options, marketers have noticed a 30% to 1000% increase in the number of email subscribers when compared to the simple sidebar format. WPBeginner.com tried this out on their website and found a 600% increase in the number of email subscribers. To make them less annoying, there are few changes you can make. At first, make sure the pop up appears only after ten or sixty seconds after the visitor has landed on the page. It is less intrusive this way, as the visitor will be able to review the information he or she is looking for.

A visitor recognition pop-up software is another approach to address this concern. This allows the pop up to appear just once if it's a first-time visitor, and they won't be interrupted every single time. You could also provide an exit-intent pop up that appears only when the visitor is about to leave the page, that is when the cursor nears the exit tab. Do not use pop-ups on every single page on your website. Choose to use them on pages with the most traffic.

The landing page or the sales page is an interruption-free web page to which you direct traffic for a sole purpose. For example, it could be used to market one product or to collect different email addresses. We call it interruption-free because there is a link, navigation menu, or sidebar that could distract the visitor from the action he or she wants to take. There will only be one call to action button — download, log in, sign up or get access — and some sales pitch to convince the visitor to do something.

You can use this landing page as the destination page, which can send visitors from social media or elsewhere to increase the chance of changing into email subscribers. You can send them to this landing page rather than the homepage. A sales page can directly be placed on your WordPress landing page using the plugin. There are also premium landing page builders that include such features as testing and gathering information. These templates will be proven to perform well when it comes to converting. The most preferred ones are LeadPages.com, OptimizePress.com, and InstaPage.com.

## Email Marketing

At this point, you have chosen an email marketing provider, decided on a freebie, and positioned a sign-up form in strategic locations. The next part would be explaining the email collection side. Always remember that your biggest asset in business would be the relationships you maintain with your subscribers. The first part of your strategy will be to create a series of emails, beginning with a welcome message. This is where you give away a free gift.

From this point onwards, continue sending other messages that will be useful to your audience. The end goal is for your audience to open the emails and read their content. You won't make any sales if your subscribers do not open your mail persuading them to buy your product. According to Mail Chimp, the average number of email open rate is 22%, with the best rate between 60% and 87% and the worst being between 1% and 14%. The factors that might affect this are as follows:

### *The sender:*

If your target audience is expecting useful information, they will be inclined to open them. Your name should be of high value.

## *If the mail goes directly to the visitor's inbox or junk mail:*

If the subscriber decides to send the mail to the junk folder, that's where all the following emails will end up. It is, therefore, very important to send just valuable information to avoid it being sent to the junk folder. To avoid even your first email from going to the junk folder, ask your subscribers to whitelist you right when they subscribe to your page.

## *The subject line:*

It is meant to describe what your mail is about, which will help the subscriber to determine the type of content. The goal will always be to trigger more interest. To figure out the best way to optimize the open rate, try different subject lines. You can also automate these messages with an email marketing provider. There are tutorials that can help you understand the process.

## Double opt-in vs. Single Opt-in

You can never trick or force any of your visitors into joining your email list. There are laws that protect consumers from you adding them onto your list without their consent. According to this law, you need to provide an option where they can opt out and unsubscribe whenever they wish. A single opt-in option will let the visitor enter his or her email address in the form you provide, and then he or she will be added to your email list just by clicking the sign-up button.

A double opt-in is an option that is used to confirm subscriptions. This option is quite common when signing up for a newsletter; you enter the email address, and they ask you for confirmation of your subscription. You then confirm by clicking the link provided by the company. This is the double opt-in process. It definitely takes a longer time and more effort from the subscriber's side. So, there is a chance where you can lose the visitor halfway. For instance, the visitor might not confirm his or her email.

Now, why should someone choose a double opt-in over a single opt-in if it leads to losing potential subscribers? When subscribers confirm their subscription, it is an assurance that your email wouldn't go straight to the spam folder. A double opt-in ensures that your emails are whitelisted and that your subscribers want to be engaged with your service or product. This process helps to weed out subscribers who are not going to be engaged customers. It will also help you against spammers. Most marketers would always recommend using the double opt-in process. The freebie provided can also help ensure the chance of them subscribing to your page once it is of high value.

## Autoresponder Sequence

The autoresponder sequence helps in sending emails at a certain time and date as per your requirement. Let's say, you decided to send all your subscribers a welcome message just after they sign up, in which you state that they will also receive a free gift, and then another message two days later offering better information. Later on, they will receive five similar messages, sent every four days for a total of seven messages.

All your subscribers will receive the same messages at the same time intervals, regardless of when they had signed up.

You might have a tough time deciding the number of messages you wish to send and how often. However, there is no perfect number in this situation; it varies for different businesses. You will find out what is best for your venture over time through tests and observations. Certain marketers will choose to send out daily emails; others send it once in a week.

To help you define your email sequence, try to understand what would be the most favorable frequency that would maintain a relationship with your subscribers without disturbing them. Maybe, you can initially send five emails at an interval of a couple of days and then once in a week. If the first few messages are sent in a close interval, it will give time for the subscriber to be accustomed to seeing your emails appear in his or her inbox. If you spend less than one message in a week, subscribers will forget about the offer and the existence of your product.

## Email content

The next and the most valuable aspect of your email is the content. It should be valuable enough for your subscribers to open and read them. Therefore, it is always important that you choose to provide useful information, which is different from keeping them engaged. Here are some examples of content:

- Mention a resourceful tool or plugin: It could be any software, a WordPress plugin, a blog article, or a book that you have read. Anything that will get your audience's attention will help you achieve your goals.

- A success story about a member of your audience: This is a very persuasive way to prove the benefits of your product. It will also encourage your audience to achieve something like the story portrays.

- Share one lesson that you learned in order to help your audience avoid making the same mistakes. This will show that you are also a normal person who makes mistakes. It will also demonstrate how you care about them.

- Share a fun fact: Entertain your subscribers with a story or fact. This will humanize the emails and engage your audience.

- Ask them a question: This is a great way to encourage your audience to participate. You can ask them about their problems, desires, or opinions.

- Announce an offer or promotion: Your subscribers should always get the best deals on your services or products. If one product is at a discounted rate, your subscribers should be notified before anyone else.

- Sell a product: You should be selling a product through your emails. This could be the main topic of your email, or you could subtly describe it within the email. This is quite a common form of promotion. It goes something like, if you're interested in X product, you would also find Y interesting, and then you provide a link to that product with the main objective of generating sales. Selling a product does not have to be a part of every email, but you should make sure that your subscribers are accustomed to looking for alternatives. You should also be comfortable with it, so don't wait too long before selling a product. You can also promote someone else's product. It could be a book, which will provide a commission for every sale. Keep in mind that you legally have to mention an affiliate product before promoting it as you get commissions.

A fact that you should never forget is that your subscribers are real people. Craft your content in such a way that it sounds warm and friendly. Demonstrate a genuine need to help them, and use a conversational tone. Most marketing services will let you personalize messages by automatically adding the real name of every subscriber. This is why the sign-up form has an option to use their name. Simple features like these would help you communicate more effectively. You can also ask your subscribers not to hold back from replying. You should also respond to every reply if this is offered. It is easier if your email list is small because it has to be done genuinely.

## Facts you should remember while building an email list

1. The success of your business will depend on how well you maintain a relationship with your subscribers. It will be your number one asset, and building it should be a priority.

2. You will need to choose the right email marketing service, which would:

    i. Create sign-up forms

    ii. Collect emails

    iii. Segment your list

    iv. Create automated messages

    v. Split test and organize data for campaigns

3. Place the forms in different locations to maximize the number of potential subscribers

4. Create a free gift, which can be of high value to the target audience and related to the product you are selling

5. Maintain relationships with subscribers by continually sending messages with useful data.

## Take Action

The time allowed for exercise: 5 hours

1. Choose a marketing service. Use free trials, or select one you prefer.

2. Create a free gift offer.

   - Choose something that can be a solution or of high value to the audience.

   - Decide on how to package your product.

   - If you run a blog, choose your most popular content, and create a freebie related to it.

3. Design a sign-up form.

   - Find a design that matches your brand.

   - Mention the free gift and its benefits.

   - Position it in a strategic location.

4. Create the content for the first few messages.

   - Start off with a welcome message, and provide the free gift along with it.

- Craft five to ten more messages, and send it the following days and weeks. Keep them engaged with valuable and useful information.

## Traffic Methods

A common experience in every online business is that without traffic, your website is like a billboard in the middle of nowhere. Even if you come out with the most intriguing content, have the best products, or provide excellent service, if no one is aware of it, then your business won't be sustainable.

Directing traffic to your website is one of the biggest challenges of your business journey. Once you learn how to pass this stage, you are good to go. As of today, there are millions of websites online, and it has become quite challenging to make sure that a new business appears as the top result on a search engine. You have to come up with different ways to attract potential customers to your web page. Driving traffic to your page means any page you want the customers to go to. It is highly recommended that you own your own website, as you will have complete control over it. Your website is a platform that can host a YouTube channel or an Etsy store.

When you start off, you will barely have a good audience size, and thus, you will have to build one by showing up where your target audiences are. In order to find them, you have to know who they all are. For instance, a 65-year-old ex-military man would not visit the same website as a 22-year-old fine arts student. You have to figure out an ideal customer profile and collect information, such as who they are, their interests, websites and blogs they visit, and the platforms they use.

It is essential to know who your ideal audience is, as it will help you direct quality traffic towards your website. A bigger website with a larger audience does not necessarily generate more traffic than a smaller site. It can only be measured by factors, such as:

- Engagement: Visitors sharing or commenting on the content.

- Conversion: Visitors turning into subscribers or ending up making purchases from your website.

- Brand advocates: Visitors actively mentioning your products to friends and acquaintances.

Therefore, your visitors are the ones contributing the most to your business growth. It gets better if there is good quality traffic as a result. To have high-quality traffic, you have to reach out to people who are interested in your content — the posts, audio, or video — or in buying your service or products. They are your target audience.

So then how do you design your website to welcome visitors?

You must be ready to interest them with the data they are looking for. Your website should include at least three to four sections if you have a blog and five if you have to sell a product.

1. A homepage: This page should clearly explain what you are offering. Basically, the information on your service or product and for who it is for.

2. About page: This page should have information about you and your business, but in reality, it should be about what they get out of it.

3. Contact page: Gives contact information and addresses.

4. Blog: If your website is a blog or it includes a blog section for publishing articles or other content, then this section is useful. It should contain a handful of articles at least.

5. Sales page: This can include product information, the service details, and the price of the item you're trying to sell.

Before you try to drive traffic to your website, make sure that it has useful information, especially if it's a blog. You should include at least two to three great published content that can be related to your product. It should have an article or video, which is a guide to useful information. Even if you're not planning to have a blog section, it is wise to have at least some good written content as they can help express your desire to help.

If your website is only a blog, driving traffic should not be your only concern. You want all your subscribers to be engaged with the content you publish. For this, you have to provide authentic content. So, what is good content?

According to Buzzsumo.com, a 2000+ worded article gets better ranking and more activity in a search engine. There are certain bloggers who would recommend shorter articles, up to 500 words. They say it leads to more comments and shares. You could try both approaches and tailor it to what works for you. You can write one short post in a week and a more detailed one every month. Whatever method you choose, it is important that your content offers a solution to one particular problem.

The way you design your content will also play a vital role, so you should use legible fonts, appealing images, high-quality information, etc. You have to learn how to promote your content because your customer will not accidentally wind up checking out your website. Like the 80/20 principle that was previously mentioned in this book, spend 20% of your time creating content and 80% promoting it. Ultimately, you don't want to be writing articles every day. It would be effective if there are fewer articles with interesting and high-value information. You can then focus on the promotion aspect of it.

*Nik Neutron*

# Chapter Fifteen: Traffic Sources

In the beginning, it is quite overwhelming when you're trying to do everything. There are several traffic generation methods that can help direct quality visitors to your site. Use the 80/20 rule, where 20% of all traffic sources will provide 80% of potential subscribers. At first, it is advised to promote through just a few channels rather than trying several at once. According to the topic, the nature of your product and the chosen niche determine the best traffic sources. Here are some examples: A friend had started selling jewelry through an Etsy store. It was delicately made of silver and gold. It cost between $15 and $50 per piece. Middle-class women between the ages of 25 and 50 comprised her target audience. Where can she best promote her products? Mostly on Facebook or Pinterest.

A Facebook page should be chosen because there are many users, which is a fact that should never be ignored. An Etsy app can be added to her Facebook page for people to visit. The advantage of Facebook is that it lets you post large images that can help people see the fine details. The next option should be Pinterest, as 70% of their users are women. It can be considered as a visual medium with a high sales conversion rate. The option where you can go directly to the product page by clicking on the image has made it very popular. Finally, she should also consider approaching fashion bloggers. Women can propose a partnership with a blogger because jewelry complements clothing. This gives you access to an extremely targeted audience, and there is a good chance that she will find people interested in her products. With just these three sources, she can build herself a very profitable business.

There are several strategies you can employ to attract traffic to your web page. Keep in mind that you should choose a strategy based on the nature of your business.

## Guest posting

This means that you have to write and publish an article on someone else's blog or website. Both the publisher and writer can profit from this approach. As the writer, you will get a link back to your page, which can drive traffic to your site. The aim is to write for a blog that has a large audience composed of your target customers. In front of these new people, you can gain exposure and grow the business. The publisher gets a high-quality article for free. Several bloggers accept contributions as these reduce workload. The main issue with this approach is that popular websites receive a lot of requests from guest writers. Everyone is looking out for more exposure through high-traffic blogs. It will require a lot of convincing to earn your spot. The trouble would be worth it in the end, as a guest posting is a very effective method. Here are some effective steps to follow:

- Discover blogs that relate best to your area of interest, which includes the same audience as yours. Categorize them into two: one for the sites that have a medium audience size and the other with a large audience. Confirm that they accept contributions from writers.

- Identify the particular topic that is most popular within your target audience. The article that you want to write for the host site should be both useful and interesting to the audience. Look for articles that have the most shares and comments to identify the most popular post. Certain blogs include a sidebar, which showcases the most popular post on the site. Use these features to increase the chance of being selected by the blog owner. You should also write on topics that are relevant to your field. You should not try to include a sales pitch or promotion in this article. The goal will only be to drive traffic to your site.

- Always observe the blogger's style. This will be helpful to write in the same format as the one that's available on the host website, as it already attracts traffic. See if their posts are written as lists or bullet points, if they tell stories, or whether they take on a humorous tone.

- Have a good rapport with the medium-sized bloggers. It is important to connect with them before requesting them to feature your article. You can do this by commenting on their blogs, sharing their articles, following or mentioning them when appropriate, commenting on their Facebook posts, or subscribing to their email list. You have to be genuine and not spam them. Comment only when you have something important to add to the conversation, and share content if you were inspired by it.

- Request the medium-audience blogs to publish your content. Make sure that you're subscribed to their list, and reply to messages that they have sent; this will get their attention. Share the kind of information that you think might benefit them, and provide them with a link to your website to see samples of your writing. Reassure them that you will proofread and send it in a perfect format. Include the word count, and use the format they follow.

- After gaining experience with smaller blogs, approach the blogs with a larger audience. They must have a lot of traffic and subscribers. It will be better to directly contact the editor in charge who handles your topics. Otherwise, your attempts will be lost in the thousands of requests they get. It always helps if you have previously built rapport with editors. Twitter can be helpful as you can follow them and retweet their content.

- Use guest writers on your blog. Making another person write your blog articles can help in gaining exposure and traffic. The content should always be interesting to your audience. You can request the contributor to share the link of this article in their network or social media. Every time someone wants to read that article, they end up checking your website.

## Podcast interviews

The rules are all the same – the audience of the podcast should be similar to what you're looking for in an audience. You will need experience, expertise, or information that is valuable to the listeners. For starters, find podcasts on iTunes store that are similar to your topic. Find shows that will agree with your views. Start contacting the show host by reviewing the show or commenting on their website first. You can judge the importance of the podcast based on the guests they include, such as famous authors or influential people. Always start with smaller ones, and use this experience for bigger interviews.

# Interview an expert

Getting experts involved always works great in gaining traffic and building relationships. You can publish the interview in audio or text format. This is an opportunity to learn more and keep it interesting while generating more traffic. You can research on experts using such platforms as LinkedIn, Google, and Twitter. You can also invite university faculty or prosperous people in your community.

Once you have a list of potential guests to invite, do the necessary research. Look for their interviews, articles written, and the shows they have appeared in. Upon contacting them, first state the reason why you chose them and how it could benefit both parties.

# Host seminars online

Webinars are like live workshops, which last for one or two hours. They are helpful in promoting a product, generating traffic or sales, and also building a larger audience. They are mostly free, or a fee can be applied. Initially, the whole point of these webinars would be to generate traffic and to build your email list, not for monetary benefits. Therefore, allow it to be free of cost and do not promote a paid product or service at first. You can attempt that after building trust and reaching a new audience. You should never make them feel like they are being targeted for some sales pitch.

As the host, you are in charge of creating the presentation slides. You will obviously need some skills, expertise, or knowledge about the information you are about to share. It is even more effective if your information will help solve a problem. It can be a PowerPoint presentation or in video format.

In order to host a Webinar, you can use such platforms as Go To Webinar, Webinars On Air, or Webinar Jam. You can register by giving your information and following the instructions. While promoting the webinar, you can share the link generated by the software. It can be accessed after a simple registration process. You will need a complete understanding of the system before you plan your first seminar. The software generally provides free tutorials explaining the entire process. But how do you get people to sign up for this?

You can always promote it through another blog. As long as your information is valuable, it will attract subscribers. Do not pick a competitor but someone whose products and offers are complementary to yours.

Use social media, such as Facebook or LinkedIn, for advertising and promotions. You can also use Pinterest and Twitter to attract your target audience. When using Twitter, use the right hashtags with keywords that are linked to your topic. Facebook's ads are also helpful for promotions. With these ads, you can focus on people who have liked your posts or pages that complement yours. This is effective as they are people who have already expressed their interest in your field.

In 2015, Facebook launched a feature called lead ads. This makes it faster and easier to attract subscribers by making them sign up or take any action. This tool has many advantages for online businesses. Google AdWords is another option for search engine advertising.

At top of the result page, you can always find the commercial links as the first two links. This is based on bidding by competing with other companies for keywords. Have a complete understanding of how it works before spending too much on it.

MeetUp.com is another platform that is about face-to-face meetings. You can become a member of a group related to your interests and hold free seminars with useful information. As discussed earlier, it is always better to try and not sell anything during this seminar. You can collect email addresses and even direct people to your website during your session. This will help direct traffic to your website.

## Social media community

Social media can be easily overwhelming so remember that you don't have to be everything to everyone. Highly famous bloggers and companies have a virtual assistant to help. So, until you plan to hire one, learn to focus on just a few platforms, learn how they work, have many followers, and once you are established, use more platforms. Facebook is a platform you can start with as it is very versatile; you can upload audio, video, post images, and text. All these functions can help promote a business really well. Look into your user demographic reports to have a better understanding of your audience.

Buzzsumo.com is another platform that can help in identifying the number of shares on popular topics in popular social media platforms. You can search using keywords and figure out what gets shared the most in your area of interest. You can also get help from tutorials on YouTube or take courses on SkillShare or Udemy.

## Facebook

Facebook has a total of 1.5 billion users, which is more than WhatsApp, Twitter, and Instagram users combined. Therefore, it is difficult to ignore the fact that it is a channel of choice. There are several features that complement a business on Facebook, such as how it's used to build a community, generate traffic, or grow the number of subscribers. A company page, along with a Facebook group, is the most common way to connect to your followers. A group creates a very strong sense of community. People will have to make a request to be a member, and this makes it more intimate. There is greater engagement and participation due to this reason. A group can also help inquire about personal struggles and needs by asking questions, which helps create a stronger connection. To spread the word about your group, you can post about it in other groups that you are a part of and also use the advertising feature on your Facebook page.

The events function can help you announce the date and time of webinars to members of your group. You can invite people to sign up, and they will be directed to your website. You can add other apps to your page as well, such as Etsy, so people who are interested in buying your products can directly go to your Etsy store. Facebook allows you to target a highly specific audience, such as:

- The users who like your page

- Users with similar interests

- An audience interested in a specific product according to location

- Users who are interested in your competitors

There are advanced functions that import emails from your mail list and focus your ads on those people. Given that not everyone opens every email that they receive, focusing on Facebook can ensure a better result. Retargeted ads are another popular feature. This can help you target users who have visited a page on your website. For instance, you can promote a product by showing ads to users who have viewed your product's page on the website but haven't purchased it. You might be wondering how much you should invest in these tools. At the beginning, it would be good to start with five dollars per ad just to get used to the system. Once you get some experience, spend about $20 per day or week, and observe the results to see if it's worth it.

## Twitter

Twitter is a great platform to connect with influential people in your field. Even though you won't get access to the big plays in the industry, you can always get their attention easily by using hashtags and @. When you use a hashtag with a term inside a tweet, this content will be shown to users who are searching for this term, even if they don't follow you. When you don't employ hashtags, only your followers can read your tweets. Therefore, hashtags are great for exposure. For attention, always use @ in front of the username of the person you want to tag. Twitter is a great platform to connect with people with similar interests who can share your content.

If you have a good article where you have quoted someone influential, tag him or her on your tweet, as there will be a great chance that this person will retweet or follow you later on. Participating in Twitter chats is another way to build connections. These live chats can be compared to networking events in the comfort of your home. You can find schedules for these chats on sites like ChatSalad.com. There are tutorials on YouTube explaining this in detail.

## Pinterest

Pinterest is an effective platform that helps generate traffic. Their users are mostly women, and the male segment is growing as we speak. This easy-to-use platform is time-consuming. If your product can be well communicated visually, such as the case with design, fashion, décor, cooking, travel, etc., then this is the right platform. The main facet of Pinterest that distinguishes it from Instagram is the embedded links on images that send people directly to the website. Another feature, which is interesting, is the possibility of creating a mood board and being a member of these boards. These groups mostly have thousands of members, and being in one gives you access to these pins. You can find a list of such groups on PinGroupie.com

They also include paid promotions that let the pins get more exposure, which helps grow the number of followers. Pinterest is perceived as a community. Users will "repin" your content if it's worth it, and if you have communicated with them, there is a chance of them liking and sharing your content. The majority of their users interact using the mobile app, so it's better to create vertical images with clear and large fonts to gain attention.

## Instagram

This online mobile app is used to share images and videos. Just like Pinterest, it is a visual medium; therefore, making your content aesthetically pleasing is very important when it comes to attracting people's interest. You achieve higher engagement when your content triggers emotions. The first thing to build will be your number of followers. Add a link to your bio section to increase traffic to your website. You can try providing freebies, such as an e-book, when a user clicks a link on your bio or caption section. It would be effective if this link sends the viewers directly to your sign-up page. Sharing content regularly can multiply your follower counts.

Hashtags in front of keywords can be used in comment sections. This will let people who are not following you find your account while searching for something similar to your product or service. Another way to increase follower count is to follow users who might be interested in your business. You can follow your competitor's followers as they might like your content as well. You can use CrowdFireApp.com to find your competitors' followers, who you can follow.

Finally, you can request fellow users, preferably someone with over 100,000 followers, to recommend you. This type of advertising can be free or paid between two accounts and is very effective. You will need published content in order to start with the methods mentioned above. Remember that Instagram is technically a social networking channel; therefore, you should always interact with other brands and users by commenting on their content.

## YouTube

After Google, YouTube is considered to be the largest search engine with over a billion users. Their video format helps in building a close connection with subscribers because there is both audio and visual content. Many business owners are terrified by the idea of being in front of a camera. If this is right for you, it could help you stand out among your peers. The technical aspects are not so difficult or expensive. You can use a webcam or your smartphone and edit the video on YouTube itself. You might have to invest in a good microphone in the beginning because sound quality adds to the overall quality of the video. Blue Yeti or Audio Techinca microphones are some of the good brands available. It's also a good idea to have a soundproofed room.

You can optimize your video using titles, descriptions, and tags. If you use the right keywords related to your video, it might appear in search results for that term. You can direct viewers to the video using embedded links.

## LinkedIn

LinkedIn could be a good platform for you to get subscribers depending on your industry. To build connections or get more followers, you must set up a profile that stands out. This platform is generally used by people to upload resumes, but given that it's a social media platform, you can use it to connect with people. You can find people with similar interests, which will help you at the end of the day. One way to facilitate this is to become part of groups. You can join them by request and participate by commenting, asking questions and responding, and sharing valuable information. You are also allowed to post links to your blog or website, just like Facebook groups.

Commenting on articles in the LinkedIn blog section, Pulse, is also a way to get noticed. Add value to the conversation while commenting instead of just complimenting. This way, people might follow you. Publish articles to show your experience and expertise in the field.

## Forums

Being a part of forums that discuss your interests can help drive targeted traffic as long as the forum allows you to share links when responding to a thread. The guidelines are to be read thoroughly before committing to any forum. If the forum is apt for you, fill out the profile completely. These forums are a community, which means that there is an amount of trust and respect people give them. To start with, just comment on certain content without adding any links. Later on, respond to questions that you know the answers to, or post the answer on your website and add the link. Even better is if you can write an article as an answer to the question asked in the popular thread, and then share the link, which lands them on your website. However, forums are not a great platform for sales pitches.

To find the right forum, Google or search through forum directories like ProBoards.com.

Website that function like forums are Yahoo! Answers, Answers.com, and Quora.com

## Social Bookmarking Sites

If you run a blog, you should bookmark it in such sites as Delicious.com, StumbleUpon.com, and Digg.com. First, you have to set up an account, give profile details, and choose all the categories that interest you. These sites are also communities, so you can share, comment, and vote on blogger content. If you are interested in publishing your own posts, submit the article by copying and pasting the link in a box made for this purpose. If this content gets voted up, there is chance that it will end up on top of a popular platform, which will drive a lot of traffic toward your website. It only takes a few minutes or seconds to submit a link to your content.

## Search Engine Optimization (SEO)

You cannot completely rely on your search engine to generate traffic, especially if you're just starting out. However, that doesn't mean you can't optimize the features that control the increases the chance of your website appearing in search results. This is known as search engine optimization. Since Google is the preferred search engine it is referred to as an example. It is always good to remember Google's main goal. It exists to serve its customers and search engine users. It helps find the best search results and possible answers to your queries. Therefore, you should aim to get the right keywords that are relevant to your business.

SEO's are mainly divided into two: on-site and off-site. The portion you have the most control over is on-site optimization while everything that is outside is off-site. The in-site features are the ones that will help your website rank better. Keywords are terms that are used to describe the product or service that you deal with. You need to choose the right terms so that people can find them while searching. Keywords direct search engines to think that you have the answer to a user's query.

Given that there are millions of websites online, there is very tight competition to rank in an engine. You must aim for keywords with lower competition if you want to appear in the first search page. For instance, the term "online business" has too much competition for a new website to take on. Therefore, you must look for similar words or phrases, which are called long-tail keywords or terms with three or more words.

For example, use the phrase "starting an online business" or "online business for beginners." They are much more specific and less competitive. Soovle.com and KeywordTool.io are some sites that can help you find keyword phrases. However, how do you know if it will work out? To know this information, you will need a premium tool, which is a keyword analysis tool. Most of these tools come with a fee. SemRush.com will analyze volume and competition for the first few terms for free. To use more features, you will need the paid version. LongTailPro.com is another tool that makes less competitive keywords. It is always worth investing in one when you can afford it. It will help you find the best keywords for your pages, images, articles, etc. You can also use Fiverr.com and pay five dollars to hire someone to run simple keyword research.

## *Choose the right domain name*

Your domain name should include your main keywords. In case you don't find such a domain name, go for a simple name that's easy to remember, with no numbers or many hyphens. These are SEO-friendly domains.

### Headline Codes

H1 code is the title of the web page, H2 is for headline, and H3 is sub-headline. The WordPress title section takes care of the H1 part. You have to focus on H2 and H3. Highlight the test related to headlines, and tag it H2 in your writing editor in WordPress. Do the same with H3. They make your titles and headlines more prominent to the search engine.

### Optimization of pages and posting of titles

Your page and titles should contain the main keywords, and it's very effective when the terms are the first keywords in the title. For example, if your phrase is "starting an online business," the page title, "starting an online business course for beginners: a complete guide," is always better than using "a complete guide to starting an online business."

### Use the main keywords at the beginning of the post

The keywords should be used in the first hundred words of your article or page text. If you include your keywords too many times, Google will mark you as a spammer. Therefore, you should verify your keyword density. WordCounter.net is a free tool that can help you count the number of times you have used your keyword. If it's over 3%, Google will penalize you. The aim would be to go for 2% density.

## *Image optimization*

Given that search engines cannot read images, you can give it a title, description, and ALT text using the chosen keywords. The image file should also be named based on the keyword before being uploaded.

## *Optimization of URL permalinks*

A permalink exists for every post or page title in the WordPress editor. You can edit this link and add the keywords and separate them with hyphens, that is, starting-an-online-business. Once you publish the post or page, you must not modify this link.

## *Write longer articles*

Posts that have more than 2,000 words tend to rank better than shorter ones.

## *Optimizing loading speeds*

You should make sure that the loading time for your website is good. This is a very important aspect because visitors mostly use their mobile phones to access websites, and it takes longer to load on phones. There are plugins, such as Ewww Image optimizer, that can be installed to improve site speed.

These are some of the SEO elements you have to control through on-site SEO. You can use the Yoast SEO plugin to optimize your web pages for search engines.

When it comes to off-site SEO practices, it's worth mentioning one important fact for Google to identify the sites that have high ranks, which is backlinking. This is when another web page links to yours. You don't want to be linked to any low-quality websites, nor do you want to pay for it. Genuine links might help you rank higher in search engines, but Google places more importance on links from authoritative sites, such as .edu and .gov sites. You must provide excellent content for these sites to link to yours. SEO should be approached as a long-term practice to have more traffic, and it is always worth optimizing your on-site elements to be organically found by search engines.

## Ad Swaps

Mailing lists are a very versatile way to generate traffic into your website, and ad swaps help you expand this method. After building a base of at least 1,000 subscribers, you can find affiliate marketers in the same business but a different area, with mailing lists of their own, who would like to collaborate. This will bring new subscribers your way. You can send promotional emails for your products, and your collaborator can do the same. This will provide you with new customers and, finally, sales that are free and easy to follow. This is a highly recommended method to generate traffic.

## Blogs

You will find websites just dedicated to blogging, and their owners will allow you to post ads after you provide them commission. If these sites don't match your business, you can start your own blog and promote your products. If you choose to collaborate with bloggers, make sure that its subscribers read the posts. If it doesn't generate a fair amount of traffic, discontinue the collaboration. The best way to start finding the right blogger is to let one of them review a product that you offer. If you have your own blog, give links on your website so that your subscribers can use it as a forum. Make sure that you update your blog regularly, and use every opportunity that the current trends provide.

## Paid Ads

Buying ads is a tricky thing to figure out. While you can guarantee that people will see your content, ads can turn out to be expensive and hard to pay from sales you make in return. Buying ads would be worth it in two scenarios. If you are just starting out and have content that people would be interested in, then paying for ads would be a smart idea. Remember that it can pay off in the long run if your visitor returns to check your content. Otherwise, you will have to pay for every click on your page, and it will be hard to turn a profit. The other reason to buy ads is if you have some excellent content. If you can come up with very intriguing titles for posts that people will share for sure on social media, then this is worth buying ads for.

## Take action

- Choose the two social media platforms through which you have the best chance of attracting a target audience. Learn more about these platforms through Udemy or Skill Share.

- Choose one strategy other than social media to direct traffic to your website. You can do this by using forums and answering queries on Quora, SlideShare, etc.

- Make a list of blogs or websites where you can do guest posts. Research on the websites you're interested in collaborating with, and read most of their posts. Interact by commenting and sharing their content.

- Use the Yoast SEO plugin for search engine optimization.

- Develop an advertising strategy, and once you have enough customers and traffic, invest in some paid ad options.

# Chapter Sixteen: Content is King

Once you choose your area of interest, created your web page, and decided what affiliate networks or programs you will source your products from, it is time to design your website. Designing a website is not just about generating some links and placing them on your website. It has to look appealing to your audience for them to visit it over and over again and even more time for them to purchase products you recommend. It is very important that your website includes high-quality content. You can find many examples of websites passing off any content as good content, but frankly, these websites are not adding to their revenue. The ones that make profits either depend on expert content creators or train themselves to become one and optimize their content in every way possible.

## Valuable Posts

The content that you want to publish should be informative. The Internet is overcrowded with users and people who are trying to sell their products. It might have used to make sense to have your own simple website and spam lots of products on it, but today, people want more informative niches of their own. You have to learn how to balance between keeping your audience engaged and making a sales pitch. This is the trick to being successful in the affiliate marketing business.

# Google

After figuring out how to make valuable content, you need to learn how to optimize your posts for Google, Yahoo, and Bing. Search engine optimization is a very complex process that includes making your content relevant using Meta descriptions, backlinking, and keywords. First, make sure that you have chosen the right keywords, that is, the ones that people mostly search for. There are tools available that can help you find the keywords people interested in your niche search for. You will need to find the keywords that are not used by many other websites but are still searched from time to time. There is a fine line between choosing the right keyword and otherwise, and you will have to master it. Other aspects, such as internal linking and Meta description creation, are also very important.

Google is interested in websites that are easy to navigate and have valuable content. This is the reason why all your posts will require a Meta tag, Meta description, and many internal links that directs to other pages on your website. This will be recognized by Google as easily navigable. All of it can be mocked up to some extent, but most of the time, it is better to keep it all genuine and have actual information that is relevant and interlinked to other content in your website.

# How to sell using content

Once your content is optimized for search engines and has valuable information, you need to integrate affiliate links within them. There are many ways that make this possible. You can include content that describes your business or product in an intriguing way while giving way to include links that are relevant to your content. This should work in such a way that the customer decides to purchase the product after going through the content. It happens when there is a balance between the information, which is valid, and the integration of the sales pitch. This method works seamlessly as the customer won't realize that he or she is being sold to, as the content is very impressive.

A second approach is to use a direct sales approach. You can create buyers guides and review posts in a way that stands out from others. For example, if you want to sell fitness supplements, you should make a review section on your web page. People interested in this product will be looking for its reviews. Make sure that the reviews you make are objective. It is not a crime to upsell your product, but having too many good points about a product that doesn't reach that level will only lead to loss. Your target audience will lose confidence in your product. If you choose to be honest about your product, customers will return to your website for its honest opinions. Address the issues regarding a product, and provide an alternative to it. This will lead to the customers trusting you and becoming potential buyers.

Creating buyers guides for customers is also a great approach. When researching keywords, you might find that, "mountain bike under $500," has been searched a lot by people. If you create a list of top 10 bikes under the said amount using an optimized search engine, Google will rank your post high, and there will be more visits by actual customers who are interested in purchasing a cheap mountain bike. This post can help you gain some authority with Google. This type of marketing is an exponential business where success adds to more success in the future.

## Importance of regular updates

The fact that makes popular websites great is that they update them regularly. When you start off, the more quality content you publish, the greater the chances of you getting top ranks on Google. Google always looks for sites that are constantly updating on a daily basis with fresh content. Creating a blog with 30 to 40 posts and expecting them to get more views will work in theory. It is always better to regularly update your site, which will help it stand out and generate more traffic and revenue in the long run.

## Link Placement

Once you have quality content regularly on your website, the next step is to place your affiliate links within your content so that people purchase your products. The methods will depend on the standard you want to keep for your website. It is quite easy if your website solely deals with selling products and posting reviews. You can provide links to your products on Amazon or other sites for sales, add images that are clickable within your articles to lead to your product page, and even set up a call-to-action button that will attract people to make purchases.

Your marketing needs to subtle if your content is about giving people more than just an idea about what to buy. You should only describe products in a general sense, and name products that may help them solve a particular problem within your niche. Adding images with links to the product's Amazon page beside, above, or below the content can lead to both direct and indirect sales. You can send your subscribers emails with links to these products. It should be a product that your subscribers are interested in purchasing or those that might be of use to them although they are not yet aware of it.

Sending them a weekly reminder can also increase sales, especially during the holiday season and other shopping periods. If you are comfortable with targeting more than one market, you may want to sell products based on the time of the year. During summer, sell beach gear, and if it's Christmas, sell Santa outfits. It is about giving your customers a choice between products to buy and pushing them into buying things they do not necessarily need.

## Content Posting Websites

To generate revenue from affiliate marketing, you don't necessarily need your own website. When you are starting off, you can opt to use content-hosting websites, such as Hub Pages, to test the waters. You can find out what works and what doesn't while not spending too much time and energy in creating a proper website. These hosting sites are usually ranked high on Google, as they have quality content all the time. This gives your products a greater chance of getting on top searches for keywords. It will help attract more visitors and increase sales. It is also a good option to combine both approaches.

There are several websites that help you post your content. Some of these can help you create rich content by editing images, social media posts, and videos that are on your personal website. Others will not provide such features but will definitely help rank your site on Google. Here are some popular sites that can help you improve as an affiliate marketer.

- Squidoo: This is a popular community where you can post articles on different topics and earn credits from the Amazon or eBay affiliate program through your content. The profits earned will be split in half between you and the platform. Payments can be made directly to your PayPal account.

- Hub Pages: This is a platform chosen by many beginners. Posts on Hub Pages can be embedded with Amazon or eBay affiliate programs, such as Google AdSense ads. These help you gain a profit, which is paid directly to your PayPal Account.

- E-opinions: This is a platform where you can post reviews, both positive and negative, on thousands of products. If the reviews you post end up being a part of a sale, you get a share, which adds to credits that can be converted to real money.

- Fiverr: This is a platform where you can do or get anything done for $5. This is not a platform where you can post your content when you are new to it, but you can use it as an affiliate marketer. If you want articles written or you need someone to share your own post for an amount of money, Fiverr is the place to find help.

- Digital Journal: This is a very serious blogging website where you can post content and make money if the post is appealing enough to interest readers. It includes a rigorous sign-up process, and not everyone can post content, but if you make it, you would be impressed by the result.

- Bukisa: This website will have Google AdSense attached to your content. Bukisa lets you share guides and turn a profit in the process. You can generate clicks, and every new click on an ad can be converted into money.

- Zujava: This is quite similar to Hub Pages, which allows the same affiliate links and Google AdSense ads to be embedded into hosted content to make a profit.

There are several hosting websites where you can practice your marketing skills before moving on to managing your own websites. Try creating content for one of these platforms, and assess your performance. If you end up generating a profit, make sure that Google recognizes your content, and move on to owning your own website. Sites like Fiverr can also help you find content creators whose content you can use to start your own blog and make money using affiliate schemes without having to spend a lot of time on content.

## Understanding the customers

Content is the center of focus for any affiliate marketing campaign; it is the base on which your social media, searches, email, and paid ad traffic are built. Without this content, Google will not be able to find your website, no one will be able to share it on Facebook, your newsletters will have no news, and paid traffic campaigns will become one-dimensional sales pitches. Content is beyond just blogging; it includes e-commerce sites, social media, etc. Each piece of content leads to the conversion of a visitor to a buyer.

The Internet is a place where people interact, share, and discover content. It could be a funny video or a product that you didn't know you needed. Engaging with good content is a natural experience on the Internet. With the low cost of platforms, such as WordPress and YouTube, even very small brands can produce content. This practice is but a double-edged sword because of the constantly changing nature of the Internet. Your brand might reap a lot of rewards associated with the content, but it can also lead to a lot of confusion and frustration because people have an insatiable demand for content.

To provide quality content, you will need a plan. Marketers always confuse blogging with content marketing. Blogging is a versatile tool for content creation, but it's only one part of a complete strategy. Well-executed content marketing will include plans about the content you will produce, the type of audience, and the purpose.

Content marketing is about understanding the needs of your audience and its prospects and building assets that satisfy these needs. The conversion of a visitor to a buyer can be achieved by using the metaphor of a funnel. A basic marketing funnel will involve three stages that convert a prospect from a visitor to a buyer.

### *Awareness*

The visitor must first become aware that he or she has an issue that your business has a solution to. Raising concerns and solutions is what your blog should be about. Use it as a tool to inspire, educate, or entertain buyers.

## Evaluation

After passing the awareness stage, customers should be made to evaluate the choices available, including the solution the competition provides. Your customers can decide to live with the problem or choose the service that you provide.

## Conversion

Those who pass the last stage have now reached the final one. The aim during this stage is to make sure that customers purchase your product and return frequently.

These three stages are known as the marketing funnel. Most visitors to your website won't be able to evaluate your solution until they realize that they have a problem and need your solution. Conversion is impossible until the product is evaluated by the customer. To make this happen, you will need to design content that will satisfy their needs.

Blogs are great facilitators of awareness, but they are a poor choice when it comes to evaluation and conversion. To convert the problem-aware customers to leads, you will need to provide resources that solve one part of a specific problem. This is known as a gated offer. To convert them to actual buyers, you need to address basic questions, such as a comparison with competitor pricing and other information. This should be built first before writing a blog. The foundation for understanding your audience's intent is to predict their future intent and which path they will take. When you figure this out, you can address their intent for every day.

Customer conversion is key to your marketing strategy. If you have created some quality content, which is optimized to perfection, you're getting a good flow of visitors to your site, and your only method of generating a profit is an affiliate program, your visitors would not mean money. Given that your website is only optimized for conversion, not much sales would take place.

There are several methods that you can use to convert visitors into customers. First, your reviews should be honest and of value. The reader will most probably buy the product if the review appears to be honest. If it's obviously a sales pitch, they will not be sure about buying your product. They may also end up checking out other reviews and purchasing the product using the link from that particular review.

You should always link your product name to the main sales pages every time. There are articles that you will find with just one link to the product in a review, and this won't do any good. You should also link the image of the product to the sales page, along with an enticing call-to-action button. This can be the review button or the flashing button on top. You have to make sure that your site is easy to use so that your customer can purchase the product with ease.

Another important factor is learning how to choose the right products to promote. This is also a huge part of converting customers to buyers. Even if you have included a really detailed review of a product, if the product is not as appealing for the money, then it would be very difficult to sell it. In case you're promoting a product with bad Amazon ratings, and you somehow manage to get enough visitors to click the link, the chance of making a sale is very low. There is also a chance where selling a low-quality product can make customers lose confidence in your work. They will see you as a dishonest salesperson who only cares about sales, and this won't be appreciated anywhere.

Finally, you will also need to sell products that give you some profit. Certain products on Amazon might only provide 1% of the total price to the marketer. This means that if you sell a product worth $1000, you will only earn $10 as profit. This is a very low standard. You should generally aim for a five-percentage award at least in order to make a good profit. Ultimately, you should always look for ways to convert your site visitors into revenue.

An attractive and user-friendly website is not the cornerstone of your business if you're not marketing it right. If customers are looking to purchase a product or service, they will seek the assistance of a search engine like Google or Bing instead of searching for your website. The design of your website will get you ranked by Google, but your style of advertising will determine the flow of customers you will attract.

The influence of online ads is not given as much importance by entrepreneurs, and this basic idea is the flaw in their online business plan. The process of setting up ads online is quite simple, and it is even better if the search engine you're registered to can provide a good number of viewers. When a customer is looking for a product closely related to yours, then your domain will appear in the search results, and you get yourself a customer. If the search engine requires a payment, it means you're not a part of a long spam list. When you are registered, it puts your domain in a spot where it will be recognized. There are options where you only have to pay depending on the number of customers who have entered your website through the portal you're registered with.

The next step for advertising is to track the ranking of your website under the search engine you have registered with. If your rank is lower than ten, it means that you have to consider other options and bring up another advertising strategy. Here are some instructions that will help you manage your website better.

## Catchy names

Your domain should have a name with an illustrious nature. It should be related to the product you're selling. The name should be simple and catchy so it's easy for customers to remember. It should also be registered with Google, Yahoo, Bing, etc.

## Pay per click

This is a trendy way of advertising nowadays. Most highly ranked websites have built their base just by using this method. This directs the customers of other websites to yours by making payments to the owner of the other website. It is paid depending on each click on the link. You should also know the format for text ads before going into this type of advertising. The same format cannot be used in different search engines. Yahoo and Google use different text formats for this type of advertising. The advertisement title should focus on providing what the customer needs. There is limited number character space for this headline, and this is the most sensitive part. If you just provide the name of your business, the customer will not understand the product that you're selling. The headline space should express something important about your business.

## *Identifying and using keywords*

Keywords help your website reach the target audience. They should be updated regularly so that there is a bridge between the website and the customers. Your website should also be responsive to mobile phones. Online applications make it easier for customers using mobile phones to reach you.

Include a review section, as this is an effective way to keep your customers engaged. It comes in handy as people generally look for recommended and reviewed sites to make sure that they are directed to the right product without any doubt. Make sure that you include your contact information and address so that your customers can reach you easily. It will also help to improve your local standards, and establish your brand around you. The local Google page should be claimed so that you get visibility in Google maps. You can also provide information, such as timing, phone number, etc.

# Chapter Seventeen: Your Affiliate Marketing Plan

There are several ways to get started with affiliate marketing. The most effective way would be to invest and be a part of a high-quality program or course that can teach you how to use affiliate marketing in the best way possible. Niche profit classroom, niche profit course, Chris Farrell membership, and Internet business mastery are some basic courses that can get you started. These courses will also introduce you to general Internet marketing techniques.

Along with the online courses, there are other investments in software and affiliate marketing tools that are to be made. GoDaddy, the most popular service provider, is the best choice in registering a domain name. Bluehost is easy to use and provides automatic WordPress installation. The company is known for its service to its customers. WordPress is a free blogging platform that is customizable and has a good support system. A good service provider would include a tool for keyword research and market samurai, which can help in finding the best websites. Unique Article Wizard is the best article submission and marketing service that can help create backlinks to the blog, which can, in turn, increase search engine ranking.

A very important part of preparations would be finding the right affiliate programs to join. The Internet has many options for different affiliate programs. You can choose to promote one affiliate program or join an established one. Certain affiliate programs give rewards to affiliates promoting a single product, set of products, or services from a particular company. Most of the time, affiliates choose to join networks because it's difficult to keep track of an individual program and raise income from selling products from one company.

Affiliate networks provide a wide array of products or services in a particular field, which an affiliate can start selling immediately. The network will take a small commission for its services, but it will be worth it in the end. This approach can save you a lot of time that could be spent contacting companies, keeping tracks of clicks, sales, and visits, getting links to products, and other statistics.

People are mostly drawn to huge affiliate programs, but there will be thousands of affiliates selling their products. This will make the environment competitive and difficult when it comes to sales and profits. Choosing smaller programs can be helpful in this case. This will mean less competition on search engines for keywords, and with fewer people selling their products, there will be a better chance of getting ahead. You should also keep in mind that small affiliate programs can also be hoaxes in disguise, selling low-quality products, so it is important to research on them before committing.

Another great aspect of these programs is that you can join as many of them as you want. If you have the time for it, you can understand the differences between each, monitor your success, and build a portfolio of good programs with great customer service and that provide good quality products to its users.

You can keep promoting these programs while adding new ones as they come by. Another important fact to remember is to make sure that you don't get involved in dodgy affiliate schemes, networks, or programs. There are programs that offer large remuneration and good deals, but you will have to do research on them to find out if they have a good history with their users.

## Take Action

1. A website is the best place to start affiliate marketing. The easiest way to set it up is through WordPress.

2. Choose your area of interest or niche. When you start out, it is better to choose just one product or service that you're most interested in. This will make it easier to create valuable content.

3. You will have to regularly update your content. The content should be authentic and valuable.

4. Identify offers that are related to your content. Given that there are many offers available online, you can monetize any passion. The most popular online retailer programs are: Amazon, eBay, Click Bank, Commission Junction, Shore A Sale, LinkShare, and Google.

5. These websites will provide you with affiliate links or an ad code to add to your site. If you use WordPress, you can add these links to your sidebar.

6. You earn a commission when someone clicks on an ad and then buys. Certain affiliate offers do not require a purchase but just an action, such as a referral signing up for a free trial.

7. You will generate revenue through the website you use. Check the terms of each network to ensure payment. There are many pay out methods, thresholds, and requirements on each website. They will also have

report systems, which let you check how many people are clicking your ads and how much you have earned.

8. Repeat the steps that finally work. When your affiliate website is successful, you will know what to do. You can now start a different affiliate site and base it on a different product. Apply the same principles you applied in your successful affiliates; it will grow your profits exponentially.

# Conclusion

I want to thank you again for choosing this book, and I hope that you found the book informative and that it helped you understand affiliate marketing in detail.

Affiliate marketing is a business opportunity that, if mastered, can generate a lot of profit, but it should never be taken for granted. It does have the potential to lead anyone to make regrettable decisions, just like in any other profession. It is just like the risks taken in the stock market and forex, where success cannot be always guaranteed.

There is a lot of potential in affiliate marketing if you are willing to invest the time required to be good at it, gather a customer base, and create content that will help sell your products. While it is a time-consuming process, it is also the kind of job that can generate a lot of profits. Despite the obstacles you will face along the way, the ultimate result will be financial independence and a long-term job that will keep you entertained.

The things you've learned here have hopefully brought the concept of affiliate marketing closer to you and helped you decide whether or not this business venture is right for you. More importantly, you should now be equipped with the necessary information and tools to help get you started on the right path toward success, regardless of how far you have delved into an online business at this point.

You must remember that all good things generally come to those who persevere and show patience, even in the face of adversity and failure. As you have seen, affiliate marketing is a diverse field with many opportunities, methods, and approaches to consider. If your first plan doesn't work out, you shouldn't shy away from experimentation. Take it one day at a time, and test out different strategies to see what kind of results you can produce.

It's also important to keep in mind that affiliate marketing most likely won't be an overnight realization of all your dreams, so you must be careful not to make rash decisions, such as quitting your day job right away or anything of that nature. You need to make this a smooth transition that is as gradual as it has to be depending on your life's circumstances. If you take it slow, the risks will truly be negligible.

Whether your ambition is to quit a job you hate or soothe your workaholic itch by acquiring additional income in your spare time, creativity and patience are sure to keep you on the right track to success. Once you feel your first affiliate marketing dollars in your hand or deposited into your account, the feeling of success will wash over you in an awesome way. Even if your first payment is negligible, it will be enough to show you the possibilities and keep you going forward. With a bit of focus, you may find yourself living your dream life sooner than expected.

I am sure that after reading this book, you now have a good understanding of how affiliate marketing functions in principle, what niches are and how to choose the correct one for you, and also how to attract customers using content. Following the tips provided in this book, you should be able to become a serious affiliate marketer with a bright future on the horizon.

Now, I would love to hear what you think! Please let me know if you enjoyed this book or what I could improve on. You can do that by leaving a review on Amazon. I'll be looking for your reviews when I come back to add more content my book. Thanks in advance!

You can do that by writing a review in your Amazon account under Your Orders.

# Resources

https://neilpatel.com/what-is-affiliate-marketing/

https://www.youtube.com/watch?v=ZjQg2G3QCwE

https://www.youtube.com/watch?v=2ETEK0ut7gI

https://neilpatel.com/what-is-social-media-marketing/

https://neilpatel.com/what-is-content-marketing/

https://makeawebsitehub.com/what-is-affiliate-marketing/

https://www.shopify.com/partners/blog/what-is-affiliate-marketing

https://www.bigcommerce.com/blog/affiliate-marketing/

https://marketingland.com/affiliate-marketing-and-transparency-a-clear-path-to-success-31029

https://marketingland.com/7-big-mistakes-new-affiliate-marketers-make-19195

https://ngsoonleong.com/low-ticket-affiliate-marketing/

https://profitfeeder.com/low-ticket-vs-high-ticket-affiliate-marketing/

https://chrisandsusanbeesley.com/high-ticket-affiliate-marketing/

https://fatstacksblog.com/earning-recurring-affiliate-commissions/

https://www.crakrevenue.com/blog/direct-vs-indirect-marketing/

https://ivetriedthat.com/is-direct-or-indirect-response-marketing-better-for-generating-affiliate-sales/

https://empireflippers.com/best-affiliate-networks-programs/

http://www.businessofapps.com/guide/affiliate-networks/

https://highpayingaffiliateprograms.com/affiliate-network/

https://partners.livechatinc.com/blog/affiliate-marketing-pros-and-cons/

https://www.affiliatemarketertraining.com/pros-cons-affiliate-marketing/

https://www.oleoshop.com/en/blog/what-is-affiliate-marketing-pros-and-cons

https://charlesngo.com/8skills/

https://www.affiliatemarketertraining.com/skills-every-affiliate-marketer-needs/

https://earthahaines.com/selling-online/the-6-skills-needed-for-affiliate-marketing/

https://www.mobidea.com/academy/Internet-skills-affiliate-marketer/

https://neilpatel.com/blog/find-profitable-niche-affiliate-marketing/

https://leavingworkbehind.com/choose-niche/

https://www.quicksprout.com/university/how-to-find-a-niche-for-affiliate-marketing/

https://www.thebalancesmb.com/how-to-pick-a-profitable-niche-for-affiliate-marketing-2531511

https://nichehacks.com/profitable-niches-for-affiliate-marketing/

https://www.affilorama.com/market-research/choosing-a-topic

https://www.chrisducker.com/profitable-niche-affiliate-marketing/

https://www.leaddyno.com/most-profitable-niches/

https://www.thebalancesmb.com/affiliate-marketing-traffic-generation-strategies-part-1-2531502

https://www.copyblogger.com/affiliate-marketing-content/

http://smartbusinesstrends.com/best-affiliate-programs/

http://mailchimp.com/resources/research/email-marketing-subject-line-comparison/

https://neilpatel.com/what-is-affiliate-marketing/

https://shanebarker.com/blog/affiliate-marketing-strategies/

https://www.affiliatemarketertraining.com/ecommerce-affiliate-marketing-better-business-model/

https://www.shoutmeloud.com/what-is-affiliate-marketing.html

https://medium.com/@KeywordsHeaven/how-to-build-an-email-list-2ee65e26d767

https://www.cloudways.com/blog/using-facebook-for-affiliate-marketing/

https://blog.payoneer.com/affiliates/4-tips-for-building-your-affiliate-marketing-email-list/

https://www.business2community.com/affiliate-marketing/the-merchants-guide-to-using-facebook-for-affiliate-marketing-02096069

https://www.amnavigator.com/blog/2014/10/15/affiliate-marketing-action-plan-5-c-approach/

https://medium.com/@mehboob86/4-step-action-plan-to-your-affiliate-marketing-success-49311c274061

http://www.myaffiliateprogram.com/abook/affbook.pdf

https://www.iab.com/wp-content/uploads/2016/11/IAB-Affiliate-Marketing-Handbook_2016.pdf

Made in the USA
Middletown, DE
05 October 2020